T0114006

The Value of Herman Melville

In *The Value of Herman Melville*, Geoffrey Sanborn presents Melville to us neither as a somber purveyor of dark truths nor as an ironist who has outthought us in advance but as a quasi-maternal provider, a writer who wants more than anything else to supply us with the means of enriching our experiences. In twelve brief chapters, Sanborn examines the distinctive qualities of Melville's style – its dynamism, its improvisatoriness, its intimacy with remembered or imagined events – and shows how those qualities, once they have become a part of our equipment for living, enable us to sink deeper roots into the world. Ranging across his career, but focusing in particular on *Moby-Dick*, "Bartleby, the Scrivener," "Benito Cereno," and *Billy Budd*, Sanborn shows us a Melville who is animating rather than overawing, who encourages us to bring more of ourselves to the present and to care more about the life that we share with others.

Geoffrey Sanborn is currently the Henry S. Poler '59 Presidential Teaching Professor of English at Amherst College. He is the author of *Plagiarama! William Wells Brown and the Aesthetic of Attractions* (2016), *Whipscars and Tattoos: The Last of the Mohicans, Moby-Dick, and the Maori* (2011), and *The Sign of the Cannibal: Melville and the Making of a Postcolonial Reader* (1998). He has also co-edited *Melville and Aesthetics* (2011) with Samuel Otter and published cultural-historical editions of William Wells Brown's *Clotel* (2016) and Herman Melville's *Typee* (2003). His essays on writers such as Frances Harper, Pauline Hopkins, Edgar Allan Poe, Sandra Cisneros, and James Fenimore Cooper have appeared in *American Literature, PMLA, J19, African American Review, ELH*, and elsewhere. His essay, "Whence Come You, Queequeg?" won the Foerster Prize for best essay in *American Literature* in 2006 and his essay "Keeping Her Distance: Cisneros, Dickinson, and the Politics of Private Enjoyment" won the Parker Prize for best essay in *PMLA* in 2002.

The Value of Herman Melville

Geoffrey Sanborn
Amherst College

CAMBRIDGE
UNIVERSITY PRESS

University Printing House, Cambridge CB2 8BS, United Kingdom

One Liberty Plaza, 20th Floor, New York, NY 10006, USA

477 Williamstown Road, Port Melbourne, VIC 3207, Australia

314-321, 3rd Floor, Plot 3, Splendor Forum, Jasola District Centre, New Delhi - 110025, India

79 Anson Road, #06-04/06, Singapore 079906

Cambridge University Press is part of the University of Cambridge.

It furthers the University's mission by disseminating knowledge in the pursuit of education, learning and research at the highest international levels of excellence.

www.cambridge.org
Information on this title: www.cambridge.org/9781108452915
DOI: 10.1017/9781108610520

© Geoffrey Sanborn 2018

First published 2018

A catalogue record for this publication is available from the British Library

Library of Congress Cataloging in Publication data
Names: Sanborn, Geoffrey, author.
Title: The value of Herman Melville / Geoffrey Sanborn.
Description: Cambridge ; New York, NY : Cambridge University Press, 2018. |
    Includes bibliographical references and index.
Identifiers: LCCN 2018012843| ISBN 9781108471442 (hardback) | ISBN
    9781108452915 (paperback)
Subjects: LCSH: Melville, Herman, 1819–1891—Criticism and interpretation. |
    Melville, Herman, 1819–1891—Appreciation. | Melville, Herman,
    1819–1891—Influence. | BISAC: LITERARY CRITICISM / American / General.
Classification: LCC PS2387 .S196 2018 | DDC 813/.3—dc23 LC record available
at https://lccn.loc.gov/2018012843

ISBN 978-1-108-47144-2 Hardback
ISBN 978-1-108-45291-5 Paperback

To Colin, Eli, and Calvin

Contents

Acknowledgments

"Stories get to be written in different ways," Flannery O'Connor writes in an April 1960 letter about *The Violent Bear It Away*, "but this particular story was discovered in the process of finding out what I was able to make live." That's pretty much how this book got to be written too. In the early stages of the process, I drew on conversations with Sarah Towers, Colin Sanborn, Jim Shepard, Karen Shepard, Ray Ryan, and my colleagues in the Amherst College English Department; I drew, as well, on the example of Warner Berthoff's *The Example of Melville* and the evergreen influence of Michael Colacurcio, my graduate school advisor. As the process advanced, I drew on the co-creative energies of the students in my 2015–16 classes, "Narratives of Suffering," "American Extravaganzas," "Reading the Novel," and "Literature and the Nonhuman World." Finally, during the actual writing of the book, I was lucky enough to be able to draw on the inventive intelligence of Alicia Christoff, without whom this particular story would not have been discovered. I am grateful to you all.

Introduction

Look, whether we're young, or we're all grown up and just starting
out, or we're older and getting so old there's not much time left, we're
human beings – we're looking for company, and we're looking for
understanding: someone who reminds us that we're not alone, and
someone who wonders out loud about things that happen in this life,
the way we do when we're walking or sitting or driving, and thinking
things over.

—William Carlos Williams

It is impossible to talk or to write without apparently throwing oneself
helplessly open; the Invulnerable Knight wears his visor down.

—Melville, *Pierre*

Sometime in the early 1870s, an English woman came aboard a trad-
ing schooner anchored off the Samoan island of Apia. "I have brought
you some books," she said to the captain, "and among them are three
volumes by an American writer – Herman Melville. It is called 'The
Whale,' and it is the strangest, wildest, and saddest story I have ever
read." According to Louis Becke, a sailor on the schooner, the captain
read it to the ship's company "from beginning to end," and "although
he would stop now and again, and enter into metaphysical matters,
we forgave him, for we knew that he too, like us, was fascinated with
mad Captain Ahab and brave mate Starbuck and the rest of the ill-
fated crew of the 'Pequod.'"[1]

I like Becke's anecdote for a lot of reasons, but the main one is
that it returns us, imaginatively, to a time when Melville had almost
no visibility and absolutely no prestige, when it was possible to open
Moby-Dick (or, in its British edition, *The Whale*) with no expectations – or, even better, to open it knowing only that the person who
read it before you had thought it the strangest, wildest, and saddest
story she had ever read. These days, most readers approach Melville

with an overpowering awareness of his monumental cultural status. They view him, accordingly, with a mixture of deference and resentment, as if he were a commodore of world literature, standing in full dress on the quarter-deck of the canon. Because they take his value for granted, as something to be either propped up or torn down, they do not experience it on the fly, moment to moment, in the act of reading and its dream-like aftermath. They never get into him; he never gets into them.[2]

But what if we did not take his value for granted? What if we were to open the books that bear his name in something like the anticipatory state of the captain on the schooner anchored off Samoa? What value, or values, might those books have for us? What kinds of thoughts might they stimulate? What kinds of feelings might they evoke? What might we say, upon handing those books to someone else, as an initial, initiating description of them?

These are the kinds of questions that have motivated the writing of this book. They have been on my mind for much longer than the period of this book's composition, however, because they have accompanied me into every one of the classes in which I have taught Melville's works over the last twenty-five years. What I have tried to create in those classrooms is an atmosphere that makes it possible for students to approach *Moby-Dick*, in particular, with the kind of idle, flexible interest that they bring to most of the other things they read. *Moby-Dick* wasn't meant, I tell them, to be a rigorous, depleting experience, a triathlon for the housebound. It was meant to be a stimulant to thought and feeling; it was meant to make your mind a more interesting and enjoyable place. If the prospect of reading it makes you feel even a little bit daunted, I say to them, you should try to clear your mind of expectations, open it up, and listen with nothing more than ordinary human curiosity to the voice that begins speaking to you. That voice asks to be called Ishmael, but it doesn't limit itself to the consciousness of that character; it roams at will around and beyond the *Pequod*. What it wants above all else is to be in a meaningful relationship with you, and it will do almost anything – tell jokes, coin words, switch genres, change moods, share dreams, kill characters, hint at blasphemies, fly into rhapsodies, go spinning off into the ether of philosophical speculation – in order to make that happen. *Moby-Dick* isn't about the Problem of the Universe, as one of its reviewers derisively suggested; it's about the effort to think about the Problem of the Universe in the company of another mind, the effort to feel, in the deepest recesses of your consciousness, at least temporarily unalone. Nothing is solved when the *Pequod* goes down, but you and Ishmael are still miraculously afloat.[3]

When I made the above argument in a magazine article over a decade ago, a newspaper columnist thought I was saying that *Moby-Dick* was "overrated."[4] After quoting passages from my article in which I had written that the point of reading the book was not "to seek out [its] cleverly hidden meanings," that "the secret ... is that there *is* no secret," he declared that "most of us 'un-academics' who have read and savored *Moby-Dick* would argue that Melville's message is far deeper and, in fact, more ominous, than Sanborn would have us believe."[5] Literary value resided, for this columnist, in the message, and the message of *Moby-Dick* was rated on the basis of its depth – size, weight, inaccessibility – and ominousness.

The columnist imagined that academics thought differently, but in fact a great many of them did, and still do, share his perspective.[6] This book has been written in the hope that it is possible to get both first-time readers of Melville and multiple-time readers of Melville, inside and outside the academy, to occupy, provisionally, a different perspective, one in which an unominous earnestness ("It is called 'The Whale,' and it is the strangest, wildest, and saddest story I have ever read") invites a seriously playful engagement with a strange, wild, sad writer.

Who was this writer? He was born in New York City on August 1, 1819, the third child of Allan Melvill, an importer of luxury French goods, and Maria Gansevoort, the grandchild – like her husband – of a distinguished Revolutionary War officer.[7] Herman's first eleven years were spent in relative ease and privilege. Then, in the fall of 1830, his father went bankrupt and moved the family to Albany, New York. The following winter, his father fell ill after a trip on a cold night from New York City to Albany, overworked himself, grew more and more sick, and finally lost his sanity. In January 1832, when Herman was twelve, he died.

Herman, who had been removed from school for financial reasons in October 1831, spent the next few years working a variety of jobs in and around Albany and Pittsfield, Massachusetts.[8] He turned eighteen in the midst of the nation's first major economic collapse, the Panic of 1837, and struggled, from that point on, to find work. In June 1839, after having tried and failed to find work on the Erie Canal, he signed on for a merchant voyage from New York City to Liverpool and back. In December 1840, after having tried and failed to find work in the frontier town of Galena, Illinois, he signed on to a whaler for a four-year voyage to the Pacific.

A year and a half into his whaling voyage, he decided to jump ship. In July 1842, while on shore leave on the Marquesan island of Nuku Hiva, he and a shipmate disappeared into the interior. A month later, he was picked up by an Australian whaler in a bay controlled by the supposedly cannibalistic Taipi and embarked on a very loosely captained whaling cruise, which resulted in a mutiny. In Tahiti, which had just come under French control, he and the other mutineers were placed in a very loosely guarded jail, from which he soon escaped. He then signed on for another whaling voyage, which took him to Hawaii, where, for a while, he clerked in a store and set up pins in a bowling alley. In August 1843, he enlisted in the navy. His voyage on the USS *United States* took him around Cape Horn, with stops at various harbors in South America, and ended with his discharge, in Boston, in October 1844. He still had no discernible economic future.

So he started writing. In his first book, *Typee* (1846), he recounted, in an exaggerated form, his sojourn among the Taipi on Nuku Hiva. The book's success led to the writing of a sequel, *Omoo* (1847), which covered, in a similarly exaggerated form, his experiences in Tahiti. Irritated by the limitations of the travel-narrative genre and by the unwillingness of some reviewers to believe that any of this had ever happened, he flung himself into the composition of *Mardi* (1849), in which a voyage in search of a lost maiden in an imaginary

Pacific archipelago becomes a vehicle for various literary experiments, philosophical discourses, and political commentaries. Chastened by the negative reviews and in need of money – he had married Elizabeth Shaw in 1847 and their first child, Malcolm, was born in early 1849 – he wrote, in the space of four months, a pair of fictionalized travel narratives, *Redburn* (1849) and *White-Jacket* (1850), based, respectively, on his Liverpool trip and his year in the navy.

He began his next book, a narrative of a whaling voyage, in early 1850. At a picnic that summer in Stockbridge, Massachusetts – near Pittsfield, Massachusetts, where he had recently bought a home – he met Nathaniel Hawthorne, who was about to become famous, later that year, as the author of *The Scarlet Letter*. At least in part as a result of that meeting and the subsequent development of what would become, on Melville's end, a highly ardent friendship, Melville ramped up his ambitions for the book that he was then writing. In October 1851, he published *Moby-Dick*.

It was all downhill from there. The many negative reviews of *Moby-Dick* added bitterness and disgust to the reservoir of intense thoughts and feelings out of which he was composing *Pierre* (1852), a manic, soothsaying tale of virtuously intended incest. The reviews were horrific; one was entitled – capitals in original – "HERMAN MELVILLE CRAZY."[9] He turned to writing stories that he could sell to magazines, some of which he later published in *The Piazza Tales* (1856). Just before that collection appeared, he published the willfully commonplace *Israel Potter* (1855); just afterwards, he published the willfully esoteric *The Confidence-Man* (1857). He would never publish a work of prose fiction again. He took a job at the custom house in New York City and devoted himself to poetry, a devotion that yielded *Battle-Pieces* (1866), a collection of Civil War poems; *Clarel* (1876), a nearly 18,000-line poem on modern pilgrims in the Holy Land; and two privately printed volumes: *John Marr and Other Sailors* (1888) and *Timoleon* (1891). He died in September 1891, almost entirely forgotten by the reading public.

In the 1920s, a surge of interest in him led to the publication of *Billy Budd*, which had been found in his desk after his death, as well as the republication of the ten works that had appeared between

1846 and 1857. That interest-surge, which goes by the name of the Melville Revival, grew in strength in the 1930s, and by the 1940s, he was fully installed in the American literary canon. That is, as I have said, the cultural context in which most readers encounter him now, a context that suffuses his works with an already-assigned and mystified value, a context that I would very much like to move beyond.

I offer, in the twelve brief chapters that follow, a necessarily subjective account of where I imagine that it is most possible for readers of all kinds to find value in Melville. I have not felt the need to do justice, in this account, to everything that Melville wrote; I have, for example, quoted only one word from *Clarel*, the most madly earnest and singular of all of his madly earnest and singular works. I have felt the need, instead, to suggest to people who are about to read or reread one of Melville's major works – *Moby-Dick*, "Bartleby," "Benito Cereno," and *Billy Budd* – what that experience might be like, how it might be informed by everything else that Melville wrote, and where they might go next if something in one of those works strikes home.

The methodology of this book is best captured by the following passage from Marilynne Robinson's *Housekeeping*, in which the narrator describes the relationship between a "magisterial woman" in Fingerbone, Idaho, and her two fatherless daughters. "She was constant as daylight," the narrator writes,

> and she would be unremarked as daylight, just to watch the calm
> inwardness of their faces. What was it like. One evening one
> summer she went out to the garden. The earth in the rows was
> light and soft as cinders, pale clay yellow, and the trees and plants
> were ripe, ordinary green and full of comfortable rustlings. And
> above the pale earth and bright trees the sky was the dark blue of
> ashes. As she knelt in the rows she heard the hollyhocks thump
> against the shed wall. She felt the hair lifted from her neck by a
> swift, watery wind, and she saw the trees fill with wind and heard
> their trunks creak like masts. She burrowed her hand under a
> potato plant and felt gingerly for the new potatoes in their dry net

of roots, smooth as eggs. She put them in her apron and walked
back to the house thinking, what have I seen, what have I seen.
The earth and the sky and the garden, not as they always are. And
she saw her daughters' faces not as they always were, or as other
people's were, and she was quiet and aloof and watchful, not to
startle the strangeness away.[10]

So as not to startle the strangeness away, I have presented many passages from Melville's works at length, gathering them in a metaphor-
ical apron, and thinking, in doing so, "what have I seen, what have
I seen." So as not to startle the strangeness away, I have kept to a
minimum my references to Melville scholarship. So as not to startle
the strangeness away, I have written the book in a way that is at least
a little strange in its own right, in a way that is highly responsive –
maybe even, as Melville puts it, "helplessly open" – to the ongoing
movement of thoughts and feelings.

In Cormac McCarthy's post-apocalyptic *The Road*, the father
stands

in the charred ruins of a library where blackened books lay in
pools of water. Shelves tipped over. Some rage at the lies arranged
in their thousands row on row. He picked up one of the books and
thumbed through the heavy bloated pages. He'd not have thought
the value of the smallest thing predicated on a world to come....
He let the book fall and took a last look around and made his way
out into the cold gray light.[11]

Value is, McCarthy reminds us, a fragile thing. The value of a book
is an especially fragile thing, because the future on which its value
is predicated is not only the planetary future but, more immediately,
the future that each of its readers provides for it. One of the vital
functions of criticism is to help to make matches between readers
and books, to give those books a future that will allow their value to
evolve and to give those readers a past from which a sense of value
can be drawn.[12] The crucial context for that match-making activity
is a recognition of, in the words of the psychoanalytic theorist Adam

Phillips, "how precarious our love of life is."[13] Why read? Why write? Always, primarily, because one wants to be able to care more about this life – about, in David Foster Wallace's words, this "tragic adventure" that "none of [us] signed up for."[14] No one knows what is coming next or how to bear it. Everyone needs a sense of the value of what has come before.

I Living the Experience

[Melville] has very keen perceptive power, but what astonishes me is
that his eyes are not large & deep – He seems to see every thing very
accurately & how he can do so with his small eyes, I cannot tell....
When conversing, he is full of gesture and force, and loses himself in
his subject. There is no grace or polish. Once in a while his animation
gives place to a singularly quiet expression out of these eyes, to which
I have objected – an indrawn, dim look, but which at the same time
makes you feel that he is at that instant taking deepest note of what
is before him – It is a strange, lazy glance, but with a power in it quite
unique – It does not seem to penetrate through you, but to take you
into himself.

—Sophia Hawthorne

In three minutes she was deep in a very difficult, very classical fugue
in A, and over her face came a queer remote impersonal expression
of complete absorption and anxious satisfaction. Now she stumbled;
now she faltered and had to play the same bar twice over, but an
invisible line seemed to string the notes together, from which rose
a shape, a building. She was so far absorbed in this work, for it was
really difficult to find how all these sounds should stand together, and
drew upon the whole of her faculties, that she never heard a knock at
the door.

—Virginia Woolf

When is an artwork valuable? For the critic Raymond Williams, it
is when "[s]omething is coming through," when there is a "substantial communication of experience from one organism to another."
On what does such communication depend? On "the artist's actual
ability to live the experience." "By living the experience," Williams
goes on to say, "we mean that, whether or not it has been previously
recorded, the artist has literally made it part of himself, so deeply
that his whole energy is available to describe it and transmit it to
others."[1]

The usefulness of Williams's theory – or, more exactly, Williams's nicely phrased version of an argument that others have made – is that it enables us to begin our explorations at a point that is prior to writing but not subsumed within a cultural or biographical narrative. Rather than address ourselves solely to Melville's texts, as if they appeared out of nowhere, or to their cultural/biographical context, as if they could be securely contained by and referred to a history of some kind, we can dive in at the point where Melville plunges into his subject, where he perceives (L. *per-* + *capere*, thoroughly grasps or takes in) what he is about to express.[2]

Here is a passage from *The Confidence-Man* in which we can sense the degree to which he is capable of living an experience as he describes it:

> [J]ust then the boat touched at a houseless landing, scooped, as by a land-slide, out of sombre forests; back through which led a road, the sole one, which, from its narrowness, and its being walled up with story on story of dusk, matted foliage, presented the vista of some cavernous old gorge in a city, like haunted Cock Lane in London. Issuing from that road, and crossing that landing, there stooped his shaggy form in the door-way, and entered the ante-cabin, with a step so burdensome that shot seemed in his pockets, a kind of invalid Titan in homespun; his beard blackly pendant, like the Carolina-moss, and dank with cypress dew; his countenance tawny and shadowy as an iron-ore country in a clouded day.[3]

The movement in these sentences is almost dizzyingly rapid. We begin at a specific nick of time ("Just then") and are swiftly thrust forward, by means of the word "scooped," into a momentarily uncertain action (what has been scooped? who scooped it?) that resolves into an image of a clearing. Once that image is in place, the depth of field begins to expand by means of a phrase, "back through which," that draws our attention toward something that is about to appear in the background: a road. With the materialization of the road comes a simile ("like haunted Cock Lane in London") that deepens the description's resonance and suspends its forward motion. When that motion resumes, it is with a vengeance: a breeze of verbs – "issuing," "crossing," "stooped," "entered" – builds, and within that amplifying field of energy, an active human subject appears, first, mysteriously, as a "shaggy form," then, more elaborately, as "a kind of invalid Titan in homespun." His simile-enriched beard comes into view ("like the Carolina-moss, and dank with cypress dew"), followed by his simile-enriched countenance ("as an iron-ore country in a clouded day") – and then he is with us, a character on the steamboat *Fidèle*, about to play a part in a brief drama with the confidence man.

The pleasure of Melville's writing derives, in large part, from passages like these. There is no structural or thematic reason for investing his energies here; he is just calling it like he sees it, and he sees it, with a particularizing vividness and an extraordinary imaginative speed, as a series of parts unfolding into an atmospheric impression of a whole. This is, I think, why earlier critics so frequently describe him as being – in Alfred Kazin's words – "somehow in tune with [the world]"; at its best, Melville's writing, like the world to which it testifies, is in a continual process of resolution, ceaselessly hinting at things that are too ineffable to capture and too attractive not to pursue.[4]

Here is another example. In *White-Jacket*, we are told that the cold-blooded ship's surgeon, Cadwallader Cuticle, keeps in his cabin a plaster cast of

> the head of an elderly woman, with an aspect singularly gentle and meek, but at the same time wonderfully expressive of a gnawing sorrow, never to be relieved. You would almost have thought it the face of some abbess, for some unspeakable crime voluntarily sequestered from human society, and leading a life of agonized penitence without hope; so marvelously sad and tearfully pitiable was this head. But when you first beheld it, no such emotions ever crossed your mind. All your eyes and all your horrified soul were fast fascinated and frozen by the sight of a hideous,

crumpled horn, like that of a ram, downward growing out from the forehead, and partly shadowing the face; but as you gazed, the freezing fascination of its horribleness gradually waned, and then your whole heart burst with sorrow, as you contemplated those aged features, ashy pale and wan. The horn seemed the mark of a curse for some mysterious sin, conceived and committed before the spirit had entered the flesh. Yet that sin seemed something imposed, and not voluntarily sought; some sin growing out of the heartless necessities of the predestination of things; some sin under which the sinner sank in sinless woe.[5]

Instead of beginning with the woman's features, Melville's narrator, White-Jacket, begins with her "singularly gentle" and "marvelously sad" aspect. Then he backs up: that aspect is in fact invisible at first sight, because of one of the face's features, a feature that must be, it seems, gradually approached, held back by his syntax ("All your eyes and all your horrified soul were fast fascinated and frozen by the sight of a hideous, crumpled horn") and then, despite its horror, given a greater weight of specification: it is like a ram's horn, it is angled downward from the woman's forehead, and it partially conceals her face. Rather than end the sentence there, however, he swiftly shifts emotional gears, first by converting a pair of verbs and a modifier from the opening of the sentence into a complex abstract substantive ("the freezing fascination of its horribleness") and then by displacing that now-abstracted horror with a burst of sorrow. "Sorrows bring forth," writes William Blake in *The Marriage of Heaven and Hell*; here, sorrow brings forth a series of darting thoughts: it is as if she had been cursed for a sin – but this particular curse could not have been for a sin that she had committed in the flesh – perhaps it was committed by her spirit before her birth – and yet the face looks sinless – it is as if the sin, whatever it was, was imposed on her – imposed by a heartless fate, without cause.[6] It is a mode of thinking that intensifies and spreads the initiating sorrow; he sorrows, in the end, not only for the woman but with her, for a woe that is surrounded with an atmosphere of sinlessness, a woe that proceeds from a sin for which no mortal being can or should be blamed.

There are obvious differences between the two passages that I have just cited. Most notably, in the passage from *The Confidence-Man* we move from scene-setting descriptions to an apparition around which associations quickly cluster, whereas in the passage from *White-Jacket* we move from a perception to an affective state to a series of increasingly metaphysical thoughts. In each case, however, we are in rapid motion, taking in materials "on the slide," as Gerard Manley Hopkins puts it, and becoming, as we do so, increasingly sensitized to an "inscape," a distinctive innerness. A "beautiful instance" of this process, Hopkins writes, "is seen in the behavior of the flag flower from the shut bud to the full blowing: each term you can distinguish is beautiful in itself and of course if the whole 'behavior' were gathered up and so stalled it would have a beauty of all the higher degree."[7] Even though one can never capture the whole behavior of an unfolding flower, a man boarding a ship, or a viewer processing a traumatizing sight, it is possible, as both Hopkins and Melville demonstrate, to approach that achievement, to gather up and stall – assemble and momentarily arrest – its successive terms.

Consider, in this light, the following paragraph, drawn from the final chapter of *Moby-Dick*:

> Suddenly the waters around them slowly swelled in broad circles;
> then quickly upheaved, as if sideways sliding from a submerged
> berg of ice, swiftly rising to the surface. A low rumbling sound
> was heard; a subterraneous hum; and then all held their breaths;
> as bedraggled with trailing ropes, and harpoons, and lances, a vast
> form shot lengthwise, but obliquely from the sea. Shrouded in a
> thin drooping veil of mist, it hovered for a moment in the rain-
> bowed air; and then fell swamping back into the deep. Crushed
> thirty feet upwards, the waters flashed for an instant like heaps of
> fountains, then brokenly sank in a shower of flakes, leaving the

circling surface creamed like new milk round the marble trunk of the whale.[8]

Visual indices – a sudden slow swelling, a quick liquid upheaving – give way to auditory indices – a rumble, a hum – which give way, mid-sentence, to the sailors' breathless silence and then the weapon-trailing appearance of the "vast form" itself, ascending from ocean to sky. In the sky Moby Dick momentarily hangs, shrouded in rainbowed mist, then falls with enough force to send the water spraying thirty feet in the air. The spray, too, is descriptively suspended ("the waters flashed for an instant like heaps of fountains") before falling back to the surface, whose creamy rippling harmonizes with the whiteness of the now-floating whale.

However memorable each term, each aspect of the action, may be, what is most memorable about this paragraph is the feel of it in its entirety – the sense, upon completing it, of having lived through a distinctive experience. "An experience has a unity that gives it its name, *that* meal, that storm, that rupture of friendship," the philosopher John Dewey writes. "The existence of this unity is constituted by a single *quality* that pervades the entire experience in spite of the variation of its constituent parts."[9] By organizing the paragraph's action into a series of sharply defined elements that are not only gathered up by the speed of the description into an interrelated whole but also stalled, syntactically and imagistically, so that the form of the whole may be perceived, Melville makes it possible for Williams's "substantial communication of experience" to occur.

It is not something that he was always willing or able to do. Take, for instance, the following passage from an early chapter of *Typee*:

The sky presented a clear expanse of the most delicate blue, except along the skirts of the horizon, where you might see a thin drapery of pale clouds which never varied their form or color. The long, measured, dirge-like swell of the Pacific came rolling along, with its surface broken by little tiny waves, sparkling in the sunshine. Every now and then a shoal of flying fish, scared from the water under the bows, would leap into the air, and fall the next moment like a shower of silver into the sea. Then you would see the superb albacore, with his glittering sides, sailing aloft, and often describing an arch in his descent, disappear on the surface of the water. Far off, the lofty jet of the whale might be seen, and nearer at hand the prowling shark, that villainous footpad of the seas, would come skulking along, and, at a wary distance, regard us with his evil eye.[10]

What makes this passage so nonevocative, relatively speaking, is not only its conventional imagery and restricted diction, but also its one-by-one enumeration, in mostly single-topic sentences, of the elements of the scene. If the passage evokes anything, it is the ordinary, nonaccumulative flow of existence, in which, Dewey writes, "[o]ne thing replaces another, but does not absorb it and carry it on," in which "[t]here is experience, but so slack and discursive that it is not *an* experience."[11]

Then, five years later, we get sentences like this:

The vast swells of the omnipotent sea; the surging, hollow roar they made, as they rolled along the eight gunwales, like gigantic bowls in a boundless bowling-green; the brief suspended agony of the boat, as it would tip for an instant on the knife-like edge of the sharper waves, that almost seemed threatening to cut it in two; the sudden profound dip into the watery glens and hollows; the keen spurrings and goadings to gain the top of the opposite hill; the headlong, sled-like slide down its other side; – *all these*, with the cries of the headsmen and harpooneers, and the shuddering gasps of the oarsmen, with the wondrous sight of the ivory Pequod bearing down upon her boats with outstretched sails, like a wild hen after her screaming brood; – *all this* was thrilling. (*MD*, 186; emphasis added) and this:

> And when we consider that other theory of the natural philoso-
> phers, that all other earthly hues – every stately or lovely embla-
> zoning – the sweet tinges of sunset skies and woods; yea, and the
> gilded velvets of butterflies, and the butterfly cheeks of young
> girls; *all these* are but subtile deceits, not actually inherent in sub-
> stances, but only laid on from without; so that all deified Nature
> absolutely paints like the harlot, whose allurements cover nothing
> but the charnel-house within; and when we proceed further, and
> consider that the mystical cosmetic which produces every one
> of her hues, the great principle of light, for ever remains white or
> colourless in itself, and if operating without medium upon matter,
> would touch all objects, even tulips and roses, with its own blank
> tinge – pondering *all this*, the palsied universe lies before us a
> leper; and like wilful travellers in Lapland, who refuse to wear
> coloured and colouring glasses upon their eyes, so the wretched
> infidel gazes himself blind at the monumental white shroud that
> wraps all the prospect around him. (*MD*, 165; emphasis added)

He had, by this point, discovered technical means of swiftly arpeggiat-
ing the elements of a description or argument; in each of the above sentences, he is able, by means of the phrases "all this" and "all these," to
compress a series of moves into a point from which a new move can be
made. But the difference is not merely a matter of technique. What he
is gathering up and stalling at such moments is, crucially, not a bare
compendium of items, but a series of associatively rich elements.[12] In
the first of the sentences, for instance, "all these" and "all this" sweep
up into a complex unity not just the billows, the whaleboat's passage
over them, and the trailing presence of the ship, but a series of dreamlike correspondences: waves that sound like gigantic bowling balls on
an infinite bowling green, a boat that is like a creature that feels agony,
a boat that is like a horse going uphill, a boat that is like a sled going
downhill, a ship that is like a frantic mother hen, boats that are like
her screaming chicks. In the second sentence, "all these" makes it

possible for Melville to intensify the implications of a theory – that color does not inhere in objects – with a run of illustrations, while "all this" makes it possible for him to add a second theory, that light is colorless, thereby establishing an emotionally heightened jumping-off point for the nightmarish scenario with which he concludes. The key difference between the Melville of *Typee* and the Melville of *Moby-Dick* is that by the time of *Moby-Dick*, he was willing and able to live his experiences in an almost recklessly intense way, to mine himself, again and again, for what he calls, in *The Confidence-Man*, "more reality, than real life itself can show" (*CM*, 217).

"My development has been all within a few years past," Melville wrote to Nathaniel Hawthorne in June 1851, as he was finishing *Moby-Dick*.

> I am like one of those seeds taken out of the Egyptian Pyramids, which, after being three thousand years a seed and nothing but a seed, being planted in English soil, it developed itself, grew to greenness, and then fell to mould. So I. Until I was twenty-five, I had no development at all. From my twenty-fifth year I date my life. Three weeks have scarcely passed, at any time between then and now, that I have not unfolded within myself.[13]

Writing *Typee*, at twenty-five, marked the beginning of what had become, at thirty-one, the life that mattered most to him. The success of *Typee* had made the writing of *Omoo* possible; the strangely autonomous-seeming unfolding in him ("it developed itself") had made the writing of *Mardi* necessary. And the writing of *Mardi*, as Melville indicates in a barely fictionalized description of its composition, had made every subsequent stage of his development possible:

> When Lombardo set about his work, he knew not what it would become. He did not build himself in with plans; he wrote right on; and so doing, got deeper and deeper into himself; and like a resolute traveler, plunging through baffling woods, at last was rewarded for his toils. "In good time," saith he, in his autobiography, "I came out into a serene, sunny, ravishing region; full of

sweet scents, singing birds, wild plaints, roguish laughs, prophetic voices. Here we are at last, then," he cried; "I have created the creative."[14]

From then on, it was as if there was a new psychic entity in Melville, an entity that was capable of living the experience of, and giving expression to, whatever was deepest in himself.

2 He Knew Not What It Would Become

> Mr. Melville is a person of great ardor and simplicity. He is all on fire with the subject that interests him. It rings through his frame like a cathedral bell.
>
> —Sophia Hawthorne

> *Moby-Dick* is largely an improvisation in which you observe Herman Melville following his ear through the book. *Moby-Dick* is probably about as close to as spontaneously written book as you're going to encounter. He gets to the end of a chapter and says okay, what now? Oh, okay, I'll try that. And then he goes with it.... The book is an extraordinary exhibition of absolute fearlessness.
>
> —Stanley Crouch

The new psychic entity in Melville – "the creative" – had no single, easily identifiable origin. It was, however, clearly linked to a certain activity: a mode of writing or speaking in which Melville did not build himself in with plans, but instead plunged in and forged ahead without entirely knowing where he would end up. After having developed, in the course of writing *Typee* and *Omoo*, an "incurible [sic] distaste" for "plodding along with dull common places," he had become ravished, he tells his fact-oriented, travel-narrative-loving British publisher, by the prospect of "plum[ing] [his] pinions for a flight" – the prospect of giving way, internally, to "that play of freedom & invention accorded only to the Romancer & poet" (C, 106). Animated by what he describes, in a letter to a different publisher, as "a certain something unmanageable in [him]" (C, 132), he experiments, in *Mardi* and the works that followed it, with a highly improvisational form of expression, in which one has only a dim sense, upon beginning a book, a chapter, a paragraph, or even a sentence, of how it will all turn out.

In *Mardi*, the results were pretty awful. But instead of giving up on the experiment – instead of forcibly managing his "certain something unmanageable" – he made two key changes to the process. First, he began grounding his improvisations in what he would call, in *Moby-Dick*, "productive subjects," subjects that could both elicit the curiosity of his readers and set him off in unpredictable ways (*MD*, 234). The problem with *Mardi*, he seems to have realized, was not so much that he had "chartless[ly] voyaged" (*M*, 556) as that his chapter-islands, such as "Little King Peepi" and "Of Those Scamps the Plujii," were too imaginatively abstruse, too far removed from the most shareable kinds of starting-points for imaginative flights, like water, whiteness, and whales. Second, he began grouping the elements of his improvisations into tighter formations. In *Mardi*, after Babbalanja declares that "all subjects are inexhaustible," just as "the mathematical point, put in motion, is capable of being produced into an infinite line," Media complains that such lines "forever [extend] into nothing" and urges Babbalanja to "come to the point, not travel off with it" (*M*, 412). Post-*Mardi*, Melville improved his ability to be "finite on an infinite subject," discovering, as he did so, how much more intense and suggestive his improvisational runs could be when he was more attuned to their gradually emerging forms.[1]

One of the best examples in *Moby-Dick* of how "the creative" could spring up and spur itself on is chapter 14, "Nantucket." It opens with a sentence signaling a transition away from the previous chapter, in which Ishmael and Queequeg are on board the packet-ship *Moss*: "Nothing more happened on the passage worthy the mentioning; so, after a fine run, we safely arrived in Nantucket." Then, to get things going, the last word of that sentence is reiterated and amplified: "Nantucket!" The reader is given an assignment: "Take out your map and look at it." Its ocean-surroundedness touches a chord: "See what a real corner of the world it occupies; how it stands there away off shore, more lonely than the Eddystone lighthouse." Again the reader is called in, this time to perceive, imaginatively, the absence of greenery: "Look at it – a mere hillock, and elbow of sand; all beach, without a background." For some reason, that kick-starts "the creative," and we begin to be carried along by a series of progressively ludicrous elaborations on that statement:

> There is more sand there than you would use in twenty years as a substitute for blotting paper. Some gamesome wights will tell you that they have to plant weeds there, they don't grow naturally; that they import Canada thistles; that they have to send beyond seas for a spile to stop a leak in an oil cask; that pieces of wood in Nantucket are carried about like bits of the true cross in Rome; that people there plant toadstools before their houses, to get under the shade in summer time; that one blade of grass makes an oasis, three blades in a day's walk a prairie; that they wear quicksand shoes, something like Laplander snow-shoes; that they are so shut up, belted about, every way inclosed, surrounded, and made an utter island of by the ocean, that to their very chairs and tables small clams will sometimes be found adhering, as to the backs of sea turtles. (*MD*, 64)

The gratuitousness of the elaborations is converted into a punchline – "But these extravaganzas only show that Nantucket is no Illinois" – and the paragraph comes to a close. Three dashed-off paragraphs later, after having waxed, briefly, sermonic ("*There* is his home; *there* lies his business, which a Noah's flood would not interrupt, though it overwhelmed all the millions in China") and lyrical ("With the landless gull, that at sunset folds her wings and is rocked to sleep between billows; so at nightfall, the Nantucketer, out of sight of land, furls his sails, and lays him to his rest, while under his very pillow rush herds of walruses and whales"), he is on to chapter 15 (64–6; emphasis in original).

Why does chapter 14 exist? Surely not to "show that Nantucket is no Illinois," something that doesn't need showing, or to persuade the reader to believe that the Nantucketer owns the oceans "as Emperors own empires," something that nobody actually believes. It exists, instead, to be a self-enclosed "flight," an instance of writing that doesn't need to be written and that is, for that reason, both inessential and resource-rich. Three aspects of the chapter are especially worth pausing over. First, it makes it possible for us to experience, along with Ishmael, the associative fertility of unfertile Nantucket, which generates, in the first paragraph alone, references to the Eddystone Lighthouse, blotting paper, Canada thistles, a leaking oil cask, holy relics in Rome, tree-like toadstools, one-blade oases, three-blade prairies, quicksand-shoes, Laplander snowshoes, and clam-spangled chairs and tables. Second, it is rhythmically, melodically, and harmonically satisfying; its matching-up of emphasized syllables, in particular, is capable of evoking the feeling that everything belongs exactly where we have found it. Here, for example, is the beginning of the first paragraph, broken into lines in which the stressed syllables – or at least what I hear as the stressed syllables – are capitalized:

> NanTUCKet! Take out your map and
> LOOK at it. See what a real
> CORner of the world it
> OCCupies; how it
> STANDS there, away off
> SHORE, more
> LONEly than the Eddystone
> LIGHThouse.
> LOOK at it – a mere
> HILLock, and ELbow of SAND; all
> BEACH, without a BACKground.

Third, it *builds*: invention stimulates invention in an amplifying, form-attentive way. The first seven anaphoras on the subject of Nantucket's sandiness and remoteness are of variable length, but average roughly seventeen syllables; the last of them, which begins by rattling off five different ways of describing Nantucket's insularity, is fifty-seven syllables long and offers the tallest of the paragraph's tall tales. Later in the chapter, a sentence on the island's maritime history builds from catching clams and quohogs to netting mackerel to capturing cod to, finally, "launching a navy of great ships on the sea," where "in all seasons and all oceans," Nantucketers have

> declared everlasting war with the mightiest animated mass that has survived the flood; most monstrous and most mountainous! That Himmalehan, salt-sea Mastodon, clothed with such portentousness of unconscious power, that his very panics are more to be dreaded than his most fearless and malicious assaults! (65)

The outburst at the end of the passage's first sentence ("most monstrous and most mountainous!"), belatedly adjusting upward the adjective "mightiest," sacrifices the rules of grammar to the imperatives of affect, which sweep us forward into a final, exclamatory fragment, in which the subject of Nantucket is whelmed beneath the subject of The Whale. Writing leads to writing whose charge increases until it "come[s] to the point," not argumentatively, by any means, but energistically and aesthetically.[2]

And not only in "Nantucket." It is merely the first of twenty-seven chapters in the book in which Ishmael relinquishes not only the narrative but his own embodied position in it and monologues with rising gusto to the phantom-like Reader who accompanies him, the Reader whom each actual reader of *Moby-Dick* temporarily personates. We vault in "The Mast-head," from "Now, as the business of standing mast-heads, ashore or afloat, is a very ancient and interesting one, let us in some measure expatiate here" (132) to "Heed it well, ye Pantheists!" (136); in "The Blanket," from "I have given no small attention to that not unvexed subject, the skin of the whale" (245) to "Of erections, how few are domed like St. Peter's! of creatures, how few vast as the whale!" (247); and in "The Honor and Glory of Whaling," from "There are some enterprises in which a careful disorderliness is the true method" (284) to "Perseus, St. George, Hercules, Jonah, and Vishnoo! There's a member-roll for you! What club but the whaleman's can head off like that?" (286). Most strikingly, we ascend from a chapter on the "Monstrous Pictures of Whales" to a supplementary chapter on the "Less Erroneous Pictures of Whales, and the True Pictures of Whaling Scenes" to a chapter so thoroughly given over to the activity of "flight" that its title is nothing but a listing of its successive resting places: "Of Whales in Paint; in Teeth; in Wood; in Sheet-Iron; in Stone; in Mountains; in Stars." By the time we reach the stars, Ishmael is so "expandingly lifted by [his] subject" that he wants to mount the constellation Cetus, using "a frigate's anchors for my bridle-bitts and fasces of harpoons for spurs," and "leap the top-most skies, to see whether the fabled heavens with all their countless tents really lie encamped beyond my mortal sight!" (223).

Part of the value of such sequences is that they signal the pres-ence of "the creative," or, in the terminology of the psychoanalytic theorist Christopher Bollas, a "genera": a gathering of psychic material that leads to "a generative channeling of interest – a concentration – which assists unconscious exploration of the object world."[3] "What I fear most," Sylvia Plath writes in a 1956 notebook entry,

> is the death of the imagination. When the sky outside is merely
> pink, and the rooftops merely black: that photographic mind which
> paradoxically tells the truth, but the worthless truth, about the
> world. It is that synthesizing spirit, that "shaping" force, which
> prolifically sprouts and makes up its own worlds with more inven-
> tiveness than God which I desire. If I sit still and don't do anything,
> the world goes on beating like a slack drum, without meaning.[4]

If the world is capable of devolving into a worthless, meaningless impingement, a slack, invariant thing, then one of our most basic needs is a living, synthesizing imagination. One of the most basic values of literature, under these circumstances, is that it can model the activity of that kind of imagination. At times, Melville seems to believe that literature can do even more than this, that it can transmit a certain kind of imaginative vitality to the reader. When a song comes "bubbling out of [him]," says the poet Yoomy in *Mardi*, he tingles "[a]ll over"; when that tingling is "infused" into the song, it "causes it so to sparkle, vivify, and irradiate, that no son of man can repeat it with-out tingling himself" (*M*, 559). Most often, however, Melville seems to be writing out of a belief that it is enough – more than enough – to

expose us to a form of concentration that "assists unconscious exploration of the object world," to remind us of our shared capacity to
turn this world into, as he puts it in *The Confidence-Man*, "another
world, and yet one to which we feel the tie" (*CM*, 218).

Not every improvisatory run in Melville's work enables one to
sense that capacity, of course. Here, for instance, is a passage from
White-Jacket in which a quasi-animated case is made for having one's
largest meal of the day not at five o'clock but at noon:

> Twelve o'clock! It is the natural centre, key-stone, and very heart
> of the day. At that hour, the sun has arrived at the top of his hill;
> and as he seems to hang poised there a while, before coming down
> on the other side, it is but reasonable to suppose that he is then
> stopping to dine; setting an eminent example to all mankind. The
> rest of the day is called *afternoon*; the very sound of which fine
> old Saxon word conveys a feeling of the lee bulwarks and a nap;
> a summer sea – soft breezes creeping over it; dreamy dolphins
> gliding in the distance. *Afternoon!* the word implies, that it is an
> after-piece, coming after the grand drama of the day; something to
> be taken leisurely and lazily. But how can this be, if you dine at
> five? (*WJ*, 28–9)

His imaginative investment in the passage is quite clearly limited:
the appositions are dully repetitive ("centre," "key-stone," "heart"),
the scene-sketching is bland ("a summer sea – soft breezes creeping
over it;" "dreamy dolphins gliding in the distance"), and the musical
interrelation of the syllabic elements is only faintly detectable. What
I hear in the passage, in fact, is something like the beating of Plath's
slack drum ("Twelve o'clock!" ... "*afternoon*" ... "*Afternoon!*"). It is
only when Melville's improvisations are tight and resonant – concentrated enough to evoke an "inscape" and reverberant with associations – that they are capable of restoring our awareness of the
generativity of the creative process.

At times, it seemed as though there would be, for him, no end
to that process. "The trillionth part has not yet been said; and all that
has been said, but multiplies the avenues to what remains to be said,"

he writes in "Hawthorne and His Mosses." "I shall not again send you a bowl of salt water," he tells Sophia Hawthorne after receiving her response to *Moby-Dick*. "The next chalice I shall commend will be a rural bowl of milk" (*C*, 219). The reference to the "rural bowl of milk" is an allusion to Nathaniel Hawthorne's retelling of the story of Baucis and Philemon in *A Wonder-Book for Girls and Boys* (1851), which Melville mentions, admiringly, in his letter to Sophia. "What was [Baucis's] surprise," Hawthorne writes, when, upon tipping what she thinks is an empty pitcher of milk toward a guest's bowl, "such an abundant cascade fell bubbling into the bowl, that it was immediately filled to the brim, and overflowed upon the table!" Peering into the pitcher, her husband, Philemon, "beh[olds] a little white fountain, which gushed up from the bottom of the pitcher, and speedily filled it to the brim with foaming and deliciously fragrant milk."⁵ By describing the novel on which he was then working, *Pierre*, as a "rural bowl of milk," Melville evokes a vision of the book as a container that is endlessly refillable by the endlessly self-replenishing pitcher within him.

He was, however, haunted, throughout his career, by the inverse of that vision. Toward the end of *Pierre*, Melville's eloquent but increasingly irritable and hopeless narrator informs us that his young hero, Pierre, is still unaware of "the latent infiniteness and inexhaustibility in him." Not yet, the narrator writes, had Pierre acquired

> that enchanter's wand of the soul, which but touching the humblest experiences in one's life, straightway it starts up all eyes, in every one of which are endless significancies. Not yet had he dropped his angle into the well of his childhood, to find what fish might be there; for who dreams to find fish in a well? the running stream of the outer world, there doubtless swim the golden perch and the pickerel! Ten million things were as yet uncovered to Pierre. The old mummy lies buried in cloth on cloth; it takes time to unwrap this Egyptian king. Yet now, forsooth, because

Pierre began to see through the first superficiality of the world, he fondly weens he has come to the unlayered substance. But, far as any geologist has yet gone down into the world, it is found to consist of nothing but surface stratified on surface. To its axis, the world being nothing but superinduced superficies. By vast pains we mine into the pyramid; by horrible gropings we come to the central room; with joy we espy the sarcophagus; but we lift the lid – and no body is there! – appallingly vacant as vast is the soul of a man![6]

The passage begins by evoking, in a slightly hallucinatory way, the process of exploring what Melville describes in *Mardi* as the "world of wonders insphered within the spontaneous consciousness" (*M*, 352): ordinary memories mutate into eye-covered creatures; unseen fish swim in the wells of our childhoods; inner mummies are unwrapped. But then it shifts: we are told that there is no such thing, geologically speaking, as a substance without substances beneath it, and that if one makes one's way into the central chamber of one's pyramidal self, the sarcophagus one finds there will be empty. We are left, in other words, with the suggestion that the vastness of consciousness, with all its trillions of past, present, and future materials, *implies* the vacancy of consciousness, the absence of a core. And I am left not with the sense that I have unexpectedly arrived somewhere interesting, but with the sense that a profoundly saddened person is operating in the grip of a compulsion to speak, vividly, the bitterest possible Truth.

3 Grief's Fire

I didn't always feel that way. For many years, I was entirely persuaded by the passage's bleak climax. I shared the conviction of *Pierre*'s narrator that in the "flashing revelations of grief's wonderful fire, we see all things as they are; and though, when the electric element is gone, the shadows once more descend, and the false outlines of objects again return ... we still retain the impressions of their immovable true ones, though, indeed, once more concealed" (*P*, 88). I believed that the world perceived by the light of "grief's wonderful fire" was the immovably true world. And I conceived of Melville as someone with special access to the truth, as, in Walter Benjamin's words, "a man who has counsel for his readers."[1]

I was not alone in that conception. Just as Jane Austen criticism has been dominated by what Eve Sedgwick describes as an "unresting exaction of the spectacle of a Girl Being Taught a Lesson," so has Melville criticism been dominated by an unresting exaction of the spectacle of a Man Who Has Counsel for His Readers.[2] But as Benjamin goes on to say in "The Storyteller," the essay from which I just quoted, the modern novelist "is ... uncounseled, and cannot counsel others.... In the midst of life's fullness, and through the representation of this fullness, the novel gives evidence of the profound perplexity of the living."[3] What I now feel about the Empty Sarcophagus passage and others like it in Melville's work is that they are not sufficiently responsive to life's fullness and do not sufficiently give evidence of the profound perplexity of the living. "If to affirm, be to expand one's isolated self; and if to deny, be to contract one's isolated self; then to respond is a suspension of all isolation," Melville writes elsewhere in *Pierre* (*P*, 295). Although Melville's forceful affirmations and denials, his words of wisdom on philosophical and political matters, are for many readers a major source of his value, I want to suggest that they are in fact less valuable than the presence, in much of his work, of a perplexed responsiveness to fullness. It is a way of being that offers, in lieu of assurance, a sense of alongsideness, a momentary but reiterable "suspension of all isolation."

Take, for instance, Ishmael's perplexed response to the painting that hangs in the entryway of the Spouter-Inn. "[W]hat most puzzled and confounded you," he writes, "was a long, limber, portentous, black mass of something hovering in the centre of the picture over three blue, dim, perpendicular lines floating in a nameless yeast." While viewing the painting, "[e]ver and anon a bright, but, alas, deceptive idea would dart you through. – It's the Black Sea in a midnight gale. – It's the unnatural combat of the four primal elements. – It's a blasted heath. – It's a Hyperborean winter scene. – It's the breaking-up of the icebound stream of Time." Eventually, "all these fancies [yield] to that one portentous something in the picture's midst. *That* once found out, and all the rest were plain. But stop; does it not bear a faint resemblance to a gigantic fish? even the great leviathan himself?" An interpretation closes the scene – it's a whale leaping over a three-masted ship in a hurricane! – but it is highly provisional, nothing more, Ishmael says, than "a final theory of my own, partly based upon the aggregated opinions of many aged persons with whom I conversed upon the subject." The emphasis, throughout, is on the process of experiencing the painting, a process that is characterized by a kind of excited perplexity, in which a "faint resemblance" suddenly arrests your attention, ideas somewhat violently "dart you through," and adjectives pour out of you ("wide, low, straggling"; "boggy, soggy, squitchy"; "indefinite, half-attained, unimaginable"). Because everything entering, moving through, and exiting your mind is at least partially "deceptive," you can never entirely separate yourself from perplexity, which means that "you" – a pronoun that refers both to Ishmael and the reader – can never entirely separate yourself from everyone else (*MD*, 26).

It is startlingly different from a later rendering of the experience of viewing a painting: a poem in *Battle-Pieces* entitled "'The Coming

Storm': A Picture by S. R. Gifford, and owned by E. B. Included in the
N. A. Exhibition, April, 1865."

> All feeling hearts must feel for him
>> Who felt this picture. Presage dim –
> Dim inklings from the shadowy sphere
>> Fixed him and fascinated here.

> A demon-cloud like the mountain one
>> Burst on a spirit as mild
> As this urned lake, the home of shades.
>> But Shakspeare's pensive child

> Never the lines had lightly scanned,
>> Steeped in fable, steeped in fate;
> The Hamlet in his heart was 'ware,
>> Such hearts can antedate.

> No utter surprise can come to him
>> Who reaches Shakspeare's core;
> That which we seek and shun is there –
>> Man's final lore.[4]

Melville's speaker *knows* what the painting – Sanford Gifford's *The
Coming Storm* (1863), owned by the Shakespearean actor Edwin Booth
and displayed at New York City's National Academy of Design in April
1865, shortly after the assassination of Lincoln by Edwin's brother, John
Wilkes Booth – means. He even knows what the painting meant to the
person who bought it – knows, that is, that Edwin Booth, who was most
famous for playing Hamlet, sensed in the image of a dark cloud looming
over a lake-side mountain a foreshadowing of his brother's crime. Most
strikingly, he knows that Booth's presentiment derived from his close
reading of Shakespeare; that all close readers of Shakespeare acquire final,
fate-steeped insights; that those insights constitute Shakespeare's core;

and that anyone who acquires those insights is henceforth immune to utter surprise. He speaks from a kind of mental bunker, a space in which an awareness of dark existential truths is valued above all else, in which "[f]ear of the unknown is cured through flight into the intelligible," as the psychoanalytic theorist Adam Phillips puts it.[5] It is a space in which bogginess, sogginess, and chronic perplexity are nowhere to be found.

Such spaces can be powerfully attractive. If surprise has ruptured you in some way, the desire to "[f]oreclose the coming of surprise," as Melville puts it in "Lone Founts," to "[d]rink of the never-varying lore" and become "wise ... evermore," is entirely understandable.[6] And Melville was indeed a surprise-ruptured person. "I had learned to think much and bitterly before my time," says the eponymous hero of *Redburn*, Melville's most autobiographical book.[7] (Redburn grew up in relative comfort, lost his father and his economic security just before adolescence, and was forced in his late teens to leave home and find some way of earning a living.) "I must not think of those delightful days, before my father became a bankrupt, and died, and we removed from the city," Redburn says, "for when I think of those days, something rises up in my throat and almost strangles me" (*R*, 41). When one is at risk of experiencing such sensations, it can seem preferable to turn hard toward what *Pierre*'s narrator calls "the Solomonic insights" (*P*, 68): the thought of "the inevitable evanescence of all earthly loveliness," for instance, or the thought that "what we take to be our strongest tower of delight, only stands at the caprice of the minutest event" (*P*, 69).

But then one runs a different risk. Here, courtesy of *Pierre*'s narrator, is a word-painting of a western Massachusetts lake flanked by forested mountains:

> Beyond [the pastures], the lake lay in one sheet of blankness and of dumbness, unstirred by breeze or breath; fast bound there it lay, with not life enough to reflect the smallest shrub or twig. Yet in that lake was seen the duplicate, stirless sky above. Only in sunshine did that lake catch gay, green images; and these but displaced the imaged muteness of the unfeatured heavens.

> On both sides, in the remoter distance, and also far beyond the
> mild lake's further shore, rose the long, mysterious mountain
> masses; shaggy with pines and hemlocks, mystical with name-
> less, vapory exhalations, and in that dim air black with dread
> and gloom. At their base, profoundest forests lay entranced, and
> from their far owl-haunted depths of caves and rotted leaves, and
> unused and unregarded inland overgrowth of decaying wood – for
> smallest sticks of which, in other climes many a pauper was that
> moment perishing; from out the infinite inhumanities of those
> profoundest forests, came a moaning, muttering, roaring, inter-
> mitted, changeful sound: rain-shakings of the palsied trees, slid-
> ings of rocks undermined, final crashings of long-riven boughs,
> and devilish gibberish of the forest-ghosts. (*P*, 109–10)

The unsurprisable are not capable, it seems, of seeing or hearing very
accurately – only of projecting images onto the object-world from violently sterile zones of consciousness. In this case, an inward "blank-
ness" and "dumbness" repeats itself on the surface of the impossibly
"unstirred" lake and again in the "duplicate, stirless sky." Then, as
if that were not enough, an inward "dread and gloom" repeats itself
in the impossibly Gothic forests and again in the compulsively
wedged-in image of paupers freezing to death in some other part of
the world. The passage cannot be written off as parody or self-parody,
because it is not strongly differentiated, philosophically or stylisti-
cally, from most of the final four-fifths of the book. It is more like
grim stoicism taken so far that one begins to hear the rhythms and
rushings of the agony within it.

    "I am sure you will pardon this speaking all about myself,"
Melville writes midway through a June 1851 letter to Hawthorne,
"for if I say so much on that head, be sure all the rest of the world are
thinking about themselves ten times as much. Let us speak, although
we show all our faults and weaknesses, – for it is a sign of strength to
be weak, to know it, and out with it, – not in [a] set way and osten-
tatiously, though, but incidentally and without premeditation" (*C*,
196). Then he grows self-conscious: "But I am falling into my old

foible – preaching." Preaching, or discoursing in the imperative or declarative mood, is something that *happens* to Melville – a result, in this case, of "the intoxicating effects of the latter end of June operating upon a very susceptible and peradventure feeble temperament" (*C*, 196).[8] It indicates, to me, not that he is a Man Who Has Counsel for His Readers, but that he is a person with what Cynthia Ozick calls, with reference to Bernard Malamud, a "wounded openness to large feeling."[9] When we concern ourselves too exclusively with what Melville's works "say," with their conceptual "take-aways," we obscure the degree to which such wisdom-statements emerge from, and are designed to protect and preserve, a "very susceptible and peradventure feeble temperament." We may even be obscuring the degree to which the temperament in question is our own.

4 Susceptibilities

> I was thunderstruck. For an instant I stood like the man who, pipe in mouth, was killed one cloudless afternoon long ago in Virginia, by a summer lightning; at his own warm open window he was killed, and remained leaning out there upon the dreamy afternoon, till some one touched him, when he fell.
>
> —Melville, "Bartleby, the Scrivener"

> As his foot pressed the half-damp, half-dry sea-mosses matting the place, and a chance phantom cat's-paw – an islet of breeze, unheralded, unfollowed – as this ghostly cat's paw came fanning his cheek, his glance fell upon the row of small, round dead-lights, all closed like coppered eyes of the coffined, and the state-cabin door, once connecting with the gallery, even as the dead-lights had once looked out upon it, but now caulked fast like a sarcophagus lid, to a purple-black, tarred-over panel, threshold, and post; and he bethought him of the time, when that state-cabin and this state-balcony had heard the voices of the Spanish king's officers, and the forms of the Lima viceroy's daughters had perhaps leaned where he stood; as these and other images flitted through his mind, as the cat's-paw through the calm, gradually he felt rising a dreamy inquietude, like that of one who alone on the prairie feels unrest from the repose of the noon.
>
> —Melville, "Benito Cereno"

What is Melville "saying" in "Bartleby, the Scrivener" (1853)? What is "Benito Cereno" (1855) "about?" And if those are not fully answerable questions, how should we respond to those stories? What should we do with the perplexity that they (and others like them) generate? What should we do with our desire for counsel, our desire to learn the truth?

Perhaps we can begin by recognizing, with the above discussion in mind, the degree to which Melville restrains, in his two most enduring magazine stories, his sometimes unrestrainable desire to preach the truth. In each of these stories, he mostly forgoes philosophical and political pronouncements, choosing instead to stage an extended relationship between someone in an uncomfortable state of perplexity and someone who is facing – and conveying the affective charge of facing – a truth that is not directly named. Something has happened and is continuing to happen to Bartleby, but the lawyer never fully knows what it is; something has happened and is continuing to happen to Benito Cereno, but Captain Delano never fully knows what it is. Both the lawyer and Delano *feel* that something, however, and they feel it with "susceptible and peradventure feeble" parts of themselves that they did not previously know were there.

This, Melville had grown to believe, is how truth is most powerfully communicated. "If a man be told a thing wholly new," *Pierre*'s narrator writes,

> then – during the time of its first announcement to him – it is
> entirely impossible for him to comprehend it. For – absurd as
> it may seem – men are only made to comprehend things which
> they comprehended before (though but in the embryo, as it were).
> Things new it is impossible to make them comprehend, by
> merely talking to them about it. True, sometimes they pretend
> to comprehend; in their own hearts they really believe they do
> comprehend; outwardly look as though they did comprehend; wag
> their bushy tails comprehendingly; but for all that, they do not
> comprehend. Possibly, they may afterward come, of themselves,
> to inhale this new idea from the circumambient air, and so come
> to comprehend it; but not otherwise at all. (*P*, 209)

Part of the reason why *Pierre* so often reads as if it were written by a person who had given up on the possibility of being comprehended is that Melville seems to have realized, at some point, that the entire project – writing a "book of sacred truth" – was based on a false premise: that you can get people to understand a truth that is wholly new to them by merely talking about it.[1] The implicit premise of "Bartleby" and "Benito Cereno," by contrast, is that if a story's "air," or atmosphere, consists in part of someone's traumatizing experience of a truth, readers may "come, of themselves, to inhale [it]." Only then, only after it embryonically exists in them, will it be possible for them to comprehend it when someone merely talks to them about it.[2]

The theory of literary communication that I am sketching out here is predicated on an understanding of the unconscious that is broader than the usual post-Freudian understanding of it as a storehouse of repressed psychic materials. As Christopher Bollas points out, however, Freud himself conceived of the unconscious more broadly than most people think. In "Recommendations to Physicians Practicing Psycho-analysis," Freud argues that the analyst "must turn his own unconscious like a receptive organ towards the transmitting unconscious of his patient. He must adjust himself to the patient as a telephone receiver is adjusted to the transmitting microphone."[3] "[T]his is *not*," Bollas writes, "the repressed unconscious." It is, instead, what Bollas calls the "receptive unconscious," an entirely different psychic entity, one that "stores unconscious perceptions ... organizes them, and ... is the matrix of creativity."[4] When Pierre is described as standing before the portrait of his father and "unconsciously throwing himself open to all those ineffable hints and ambiguities, and undefined half-suggestions, which now and then people the soul's atmosphere, as thickly as in a soft, steady snow-storm, the snow-flakes people the air" (*P*, 84), or when Ishmael's imaginary masthead-stander "takes the mystic ocean at his feet for the visible image of that deep, blue, bottomless soul, pervading mankind and nature; and every strange, half-seen, gliding, beautiful thing that eludes him; every dimly-discovered, uprising fin of some undiscernible form, seems to him the embodiment of those elusive thoughts that only people the soul by continually flitting through it" (*MD*, 136), the unconscious is being conceptualized in a similar way, as an entity that can be thrown open to, and peopled by, elusive transmissions. Through its reception of those transmissions, the unconscious can come to "know" things that, because they are insufficiently formulated, cannot yet be thought or expressed. There are, *Pierre*'s narrator writes, "some things that men think they do not know, [that] are ... for all that thoroughly comprehended by them; and yet, so to speak, though contained in themselves, are kept a secret from themselves. The idea of Death seems such a thing" (*P*, 294).

The "rather elderly" lawyer who narrates "Bartleby" seems at first to be impregnable to any such transmissions. "[T]hough I belong to a profession proverbially energetic and nervous, even to turbulence, at times, yet nothing of that sort have I ever suffered to invade my peace," he tells us.[5] After having been, for many years, "one of those unambitious lawyers who ... in the cool tranquility of a snug retreat, do a snug business among rich men's bonds and mortgages and title-deeds," he has acquired the reputation of being "an eminently *safe* man" (66; emphasis in original). Then, however, he encounters some-one who gradually and almost without action begins to dissolve that sense of peace and safety. "[A] motionless young man one morning, stood upon my office threshold, the door being open, for it was sum-mer," the lawyer tells us. "I can see that figure now – pallidly neat, pitiably respectable, incurably forlorn! It was Bartleby" (71).

The adverbs in the exclamatory clause are the first of many that will be applied to the new scrivener. Because the lawyer knows so lit-tle about *why* Bartleby says what he says and does what he does, he is enormously aware of *how* Bartleby says and does things. Here are a few of the many moments in which Bartleby's actions are bathed in the atmosphere of adverbs or adverbial phrases:

> "I would prefer not to," he said, and gently disappeared behind the screen. (73)

> "I prefer not to," he replied in a flute-like tone. (74)

> "I prefer not to," he respectfully and slowly said, and mildly dis-appeared. (77)

> "I would prefer *not* to quit you," he replied, gently emphasizing the *not*. (88; emphasis in original)

Semantically, Bartleby's famous formula communicates almost nothing. But his nonsemantic modes of speaking and acting (or not speaking and not acting) communicate in powerful and distinctive ways. "His face was leanly composed; his gray eye calm," the law-yer writes. "Not a wrinkle of agitation rippled him" (73). "[T]here was something about Bartleby that not only strangely disarmed me, but in a wonderful manner touched and disconcerted me" (74). "[I]t was his wonderful mildness chiefly, which not only disarmed me, but unmanned me, as it were" (79). "[H]is countenance remained immovable, only there was the faintest conceivable tremor of the white attenuated mouth" (82). What is conveyed at such moments is, as the critic Dan McCall writes, "not the motive of Bartleby's silence but the dimension of it."[6] Bartleby's behavior, as the lawyer experiences it, is above all else *large*. Hence the hyperbolic imagery that so often leaps into the lawyer's mind when faced with Bartleby: "For a few moments I was turned into a pillar of salt, standing at the head of my seated column of clerks" (73); "[L]ike the last column of some ruined temple, he remained standing mute and solitary in the middle of the otherwise deserted room" (86). The rumor that Bartleby once worked in the Dead Letter Office is credible to the lawyer because of the massiveness of the sorrow that he associates with the position. Nothing but a past experience of that kind could account for the massiveness of the affective burden that Bartleby has so composedly, with only "the faintest conceivable tremor," borne.

The crux of the story is the well-known scene in which the lawyer discovers, on a Sunday morning, that Bartleby has been sleeping in the office.

> Immediately then the thought came sweeping across me, What miserable friendlessness and loneliness are here revealed! His poverty is great; but his solitude, how horrible! Think of it. Of a Sunday, Wall-street is deserted as Petra; and every night of every day it is an emptiness. This building too, which of weekdays hums with industry and life, at nightfall echoes with sheer vacancy, and all through Sunday is forlorn. And here Bartleby makes his home; sole spectator of a solitude which he has seen all populous – a sort of innocent and transformed Marius brooding among the ruins of Carthage!
>
> For the first time in my life a feeling of overpowering stinging melancholy seized me. Before, I had never experienced aught but

a not-unpleasing sadness. The bond of a common humanity now drew me irresistibly to gloom. A fraternal melancholy! For both I and Bartleby were sons of Adam. I remembered the bright silks and sparkling faces I had seen that day, in gala trim, swan-like sailing down the Mississippi of Broadway; and I contrasted them with the pallid copyist, and thought to myself, Ah, happiness courts the light, so we deem the world is gay; but misery hides aloof, so we deem that misery there is none. These sad fancy-ings – chimeras, doubtless, of a sick and silly brain – led on to other and more special thoughts, concerning the eccentricities of Bartleby. Presentiments of strange discoveries hovered round me. The scrivener's pale form appeared to me laid out, among uncaring strangers, in its shivering winding sheet. (80)

The first thought – "What miserable friendlessness and loneliness are here revealed! His poverty is great; but his solitude, how horrible!" – comes instantly to the lawyer's mind only because its way has been prepared by his increasingly dimensional encounters with Bartleby. Its entrance into his previously *"safe"* consciousness is startling enough, but even more startling is the process of thinking and feeling that it sets in motion. Riveted to the spot by the force of what has been revealed, he dwells on its implications ("Think of it"), drifts into associative bypaths ("a sort of innocent and transformed Marius brooding among the ruins of Carthage!"), is seized by a uniquely intense melancholy, and then discovers that he is sorrowing not *for* his unfortunate employee but *along with* both Bartleby and humanity as a whole ("For both I and Bartleby were sons of Adam"). This leads, briefly, to the formulation of a self-distancing maxim ("Ah, happiness courts the light, so we deem the world is gay; but misery hides aloof, so we deem that misery there is none"), but the associative process soon carries him beyond that formulation, into "special thoughts" about Bartleby's characteristics and imagistic guesses as to Bartleby's fate.

Abruptly breaking those reveries, the lawyer unlocks Bartleby's desk, fishes out a small stash of money bound up in a handkerchief, and begins tallying up what he knows about Bartleby: he never initiates conversation, never reads, never drinks, never goes anywhere, never gives any information about himself, and never surrenders his "austere reserve" (81). The more attention he pays to Bartleby's particularities, the less attention he pays to the affinity between their existential situations – the affinity between, say, the idea of Death secreted in Bartleby and the idea of Death secreted in himself.[7] By the end of the scene, the lawyer has reduced Bartleby to a case of "excessive and organic ill," reduced his own feelings about Bartleby to pity, and concluded that if "pity cannot lead to effectual succor, common sense bids the soul be rid of it" (81).

The remainder of the story traces out the consequences of those reductions. Once the lawyer has restricted his experience of Bartleby to the domain of what can be known and confined his future relationship to Bartleby to the domain of what can be cured, the way is clear for him to rid himself of Bartleby while preserving the appearance of having done the right thing. What is thereby sacrificed, Melville suggests, is everything in one's relationships to others that exists beyond empirical data and best practices. Toward the end of the story, in the yard of the prison to which Bartleby has been taken, the lawyer briefly senses the magnitude of what he has overlooked and foreclosed. Surrounded on all sides by "masonry [that] weighed upon me with its gloom," a gloom that he has not felt since that Sunday morning in his office, he sees, and feels beneath his feet, "a soft imprisoned turf." Its presence is, to him, as unexpected and miraculous as the presence of grass in the "heart of the eternal pyramids" (97). Resonating, at this moment, not only with what is gloomy in the human condition but also with all of the upspringing forces that sustain us – forces that Bartleby kept alive in himself, forces that were part of the effect that he had on those around him – the lawyer touches Bartleby, who is lying on the turf, and discovers that he is dead. When he says, in the story's last lines, "Ah Bartleby! Ah humanity!", the "Ah" captures not only his sorrow for our shared condition but also, at some level, his reverence for our grass-like resilience, our capacity to keep embarking, even while "speed[ing] to death," on "errands of life" (98).[8]

The passage in "Benito Cereno" that corresponds most closely to the Sunday-morning passage in "Bartleby" is the interchange between Captain Delano and Benito Cereno after the main events of the story have concluded – after, that is, Captain Delano has finally figured out that the seeming slaves on the Spanish ship *San Dominick* had in fact violently freed themselves and that the Spaniards on the ship, including Cereno, the captain, had been forced to pretend that they were in charge.

> "You are saved, Don Benito," cried Captain Delano, more and more astonished and pained; "you are saved; what has cast such a shadow upon you?"
>
> "The negro."
>
> There was silence, while the moody man sat, slowly and unconsciously gathering his mantle about him, as if it were a pall.[9]

Something larger than Delano is prepared to take in, something having to do with the encounter between "the moody man" and "[t]he negro," looms out of the story at this moment. Throughout the story, Delano has paid an inordinate amount of attention to Cereno's disposition and self-presentation; on forty separate occasions, he takes note of Cereno's "manner," "mood," "demeanor," "air," "aspect," "posture," "tone," "appearance," "state," or "mien."[10] In his final reported conversation with Cereno, he tries again and again to get the moody man to be, now that the *San Dominick*'s revolution and simulated non-revolution have come to an end, moody no more. He wants Cereno's bearing to reflect nothing more than his present surroundings and circumstances, to be responsive to nothing more than the "bright sun," the "blue sea," the "blue sky," and Delano's own "cordial" and "fraternal" attentiveness. But Cereno cannot gratify this desire. Something more than the present is present in him, something whose absoluteness and generalizability are succinctly evoked by the definite article ("the") and a nominalized adjective with multiple connotations ("negro").

Among early twentieth-century critics of "Benito Cereno," the standard reading was that "the negro" stands for "evil," that Melville is alluding, in this passage, to what he calls, in *Hawthorne and His Mosses*, the "mystical blackness" of "Innate Depravity and Original Sin."[11] In the blitheness of their racism and the firmness of their belief that great art transcends its time-bound referents, those modernist-era critics can seem very far removed from our own era. They are not so far removed, however, when it comes to their strong desire to arrive at a bottom line, to know what the story "says" about a subject that is culturally invested with significance. Many recent critics of "Benito Cereno," myself included, have been at pains to identify what the story "says" about the histories of slavery and racism, about the violent subjugations and stigmatizations of black people. They – we – have typically tried to do so by focusing on Melville's representation of Babo, the mastermind of the revolt, whose "slight frame" was "inadequate to that which it held" and whose "head, that hive of subtlety," ends the story "fixed on a pole" in a South American plaza, "[meeting], unabashed, the gaze of the whites" (257).[12] But it now seems to me that it may be worth focusing a bit more on Cereno's two-word reply, worth listening a little harder to its reverberations, worth thinking about Cereno as being, like Bartleby, a means of gaining access not so much to the truth as to the feeling of coming into contact with it.[13]

For what Cereno is testifying to is the *effect* on him of "the negro." The shadow is neither Babo in particular nor black people in general; it is the endlessly self-renewing image of Cereno's true *relationship* to Babo/black people, an image whose unsettlingness became even more intense when he was forced to act out, along with everyone else on the ship, what had once been a "natural" racial hierarchy. As a result of that self-discrediting performance, Cereno has lost faith in his racial identity; never again, the narrator indicates, will he be able to believe in the existence of an open, sunlit space between white and black people in which white supremacy naturally and unequivocally appears. Two of the conversational topics over which "all [Cereno's] old reserves were piled," the narrator tells us near the end of the story, were the experience of wearing as a costume what had once been his own clothes and the experience of displaying, as part of that costume, what appeared to be a sword but was in fact an "artificially stiffened" scabbard (256). Much of the reason why it was, as Cereno repeatedly tells Delano, so "hard ... to enact the part forced on [him] by Babo" (255) was that he had to pretend to be himself while remaining, at all times, acutely aware of the artificiality and emptiness of that self. When Cereno answers Delano's question about what has cast such a shadow on him by saying "[t]he negro," he is not saying that a metaphysical quality inherent in Babo/black people is weighing on him; he is saying that his relationship to Babo/black people is now suffused, for him, with an affectively charged sense of insubstantiality, so much so that all human relationships now appear equally insubstantial. "[E]ven the best men [may] err," he says when forgiving Delano for his misreading of him, "in judging the conduct of one with the recesses of whose condition he is not acquainted. But you were forced to it; and you were in time undeceived. Would that, in both respects, it was so ever, and with all men" (256). The exception, he now believes, is being forced into misperceptions and being undeceived; the rule is misperceiving all by ourselves and never being undeceived.

Signs of insubstantiality – "[s]hadows present, foreshadowing deeper shadows to come" (182) – are everywhere in the story. It opens on a morning in which "troubled grey vapors" are gradually dissipating" (182); slowly brings before us a shipboard scene that "seems unreal," nothing more than "a shadowy tableau just emerged from the deep, which directly must receive back what it gave" (186); and then directs our attention to a very poor player, a captain who, "like some hypochondriac abbot," moves "slowly about, at times suddenly pausing, starting, or staring, biting his lip, biting his finger-nail, flushing, paling, twitching his beard, with other symptoms of an absent or moody mind" (188). Because the narrative's focalizer, Delano, is "singularly undistrustful" (183), we are invited not only to perceive this threadbare theatricality ourselves, but to observe its repeated intrusion into and ejection from a mind that is determined not to process it. At one point, Delano unexpectedly finds himself entertaining the idea that Cereno is "playing a part," an idea that comes "not from within, but from without" – not from a "train of thought," that is, but from "something in Don Benito's manner just then." The idea vanishes, however, "like hoar frost," as soon as "the mild sun of Captain Delano's good-nature regained its meridian" (201). Later, while Babo is preparing to shave Cereno, there is, to Delano, "something so hollow in the Spaniard's manner, with apparently some reciprocal hollowness in the servant's dusky comment of silence, that the idea flashed across him, that possibly master and man, for some unknown purpose, were acting out, both in word and deed, nay, to the very tremor of Don Benito's limbs, some juggling play before him." Soon thereafter, however, "regarding the notion as a whimsy, insensibly suggested, perhaps, by the theatrical aspect of Don Benito in his harlequin ensign, Captain Delano speedily banished it" (224). Being in the company of Cereno entails, for Delano, a near-constant struggle to reject intimations that he cannot help but unconsciously receive.

It is as if Cereno is, like Bartleby, a kind of performance-art object, a person marked off by his or her "air" as a potential source of aesthetic experience. As a result of the traumatic charge that Cereno bears, the affective excessiveness that his manner shapes, he makes peculiarly apparitional impressions on Delano. Over the course of the main part of the narrative, Delano receives from him the impressions of (among other things) "cloudy languor" (189), "splenetic disrelish" (189), "slumbering dominion" (190), "innocent lunacy" (200), "wicked imposture" (200), "hectic animation" (228), "cadaverous sullenness" (232), and, finally, "something in the man ... far beyond any mere unsociality or sourness previously evinced" (232). There's *something about* Cereno, as a result of his prolonged and forced effort to keep up the illusion of a certain state of things, something powerful enough to transmit itself even to someone like Delano, someone who has, but prefers not to know that he has, unconscious "susceptibilities." Cereno is, for Delano and potentially for us, a conduit to worlds beneath or within the world of the present: not only to the infraworld of white–black relations as they actually are – artificial, empty, self-replicating, sustained only by a permanent threat of violence – but to an even deeper world, signified by the skeleton affixed to the bow of the *San Dominick*, in which "white" and "black" people cannot be told apart. We don't know what Cereno thinks about Babo or black people in general; we only know that the state of feeling into which he has been thrown by "the negro," a state of feeling that accompanies him to the grave, is as vast and spectral as the "gigantic ribbed shadow" that the skeleton, "gleaming in the horizontal moonlight," casts over the surface of the ocean (240).

Because "Benito Cereno" focuses not on the consciousnesses of the Africans on the *San Dominick*, but on one white person's disturbed awareness of another white person's disturbed affect, it is possible to argue that it is, like Mark Twain's *Huckleberry Finn*, an "evasion."[14] It is also possible, however, to think of Melville's deflection away from the inside story of the slave revolt in something like the way that Toni Morrison thinks of Twain's deflection away from the inside story of Jim. "[M]uch of [*Huckleberry Finn's*] genius lies in its quiescence, the silences that pervade it and give it a porous quality," Morrison writes. "The withholdings at critical moments, which I once took to be deliberate evasions, stumbles even, or a writer's impatience with his or her material, I began to see as otherwise: as entrances, crevices, gaps, seductive invitations flashing the possibility of meaning. Unarticulated eddies that encourage diving into the novel's undertow – the real place where writer captures reader."[15] If we think of Melville's investment in the wraith-like quality of incipient thoughts as an investment in the moment at which consciousness begins to change, we can, I think, begin to appreciate his story's peculiar contribution to the contemporary discourse on race and politics. For how *do* minds change? How do the not-yet-organized elements of potential thoughts begin to coalesce in ways that add something new to one's consciousness? And how might these considerations help us to reimagine the process of persuasion? How might they raise our awareness of our vulnerability to being "insensibly operated upon by certain general notions" (209); how might they help us to *have* ideas, as opposed to being had by them? "Every one must know the tantalizing effect of the blank rhythm of some forgotten verse, restlessly dancing in one's mind, striving to be filled out with words," William James writes. Becoming attuned to that tantalizing rhythm, beginning to "tingle with the sense of our closeness" to the words, the thoughts, the discourses that would fill it out, is by no means an evasion of politics; it is both the precondition of new "notions" and the basis of the kinds of mutually interested relationships upon which a democracy depends.[16]

When one is "finally able to think about a previously unaccepted part of life," the psychoanalytic theorist Donnell Stern writes,

> seldom are fully formulated thoughts simply waiting to be discovered, ready for exposition. Instead, what is usually experienced is a fresh state of not-knowing, a kind of confusion.... Before, one could not even have said there was anything to learn; now one realizes for the first time that one does not know – and, by implication, that one has not known.[17]

"The phenomenon is analogous," Stern goes on to say, "to an experience most people have had at twilight, when the light is dim and unreliable and familiar shapes can be hard to recognize." Usually, after a little while, "the unformulated percept falls together into some familiar shape and one is relieved." In some cases, however, we "may be left ... with an increased awareness of the ubiquity of interpretation in our psychic lives, a suspicion that even the coherent perception, when it emerges, is an interpretation, just one that happens to fall easily into place."[18] The value of "Benito Cereno" is not only that it transmits the effects of a long immersion in the uncertain twilight of black–white relations, but also that it is capable of conveying, as a result, "an increased awareness of the ubiquity of interpretation in our psychic lives." The story would of course be much easier to take, at this historical juncture, if Melville had consistently and explicitly articulated in it an uncompromising opposition to slavery and racism.[19] But while that may be the story that many of us would like "Benito Cereno" to be, it is not the story that Melville actually wrote. For better or for worse, Melville chose to experiment, in "Benito Cereno," with an obliquely evocative way of communicating the truths that slavery and racism deny. Something further may follow, Melville thinks, from initiating a racially twilit process of comprehension and indicating the dimension of what is out there to comprehend.[20] "[S]torms are formed behind the storm we feel," he writes in "Misgivings," a poem in *Battle-Pieces*. "The hemlock shakes in the rafter, the oak in the driving keel."[21]

5 Disportings

I enclose a very remarkable quotation from [Melville's] private letter to Mr. Hawthorne about [*The House of the Seven Gables*] but as it is wholly confidential *do not show it*. The fresh, sincere, glowing mind that utters it is in a state of "fluid consciousness," & to Mr. Hawthorne speaks his innermost about GOD, the Devil & Life if so be he can get at the Truth – for he is a boy in opinion – having settled nothing as yet ... & it would betray him to make public his confessions & efforts to grasp, – because they would be considered perhaps impious, if one did not take in the whole scope of the case.

—Sophia Hawthorne

[S]ince you, with your spiritualizing nature, see more things than other people, and by the same process, refine all you see, so that they are not the same things that other people see, but things which while you think you but humbly discover them, you do in fact create them for yourself – therefore, upon the whole, I do not so much marvel at your expressions concerning Moby Dick.

—Melville, letter to Sophia Hawthorne

"One day," Christopher Bollas writes, "while at work with an analysand, I ... realized that one of my functions for him was to be of use for his idiom moves – for private articulations of his personality potential – which could only be accomplished by eliciting different elements of my own personality."[1] Bollas, who wrote a dissertation on Melville and briefly taught English at the University of Massachusetts, Amherst, would go on to turn this moment of realization into the basis of a major rethinking of the point of psychoanalysis. In a good-enough psychoanalytic relationship, Bollas writes, "the spirit of the analyst's comments links up with the patient's affect to establish *movement*."[2] What moves, at such moments, is the patient's "idiom," his or her specific repertoire of ways of engaging with the world, and what it moves towards is not "an expression of inner content," as in the classical psychoanalytic model, but opportunity after opportunity after opportunity for self-elaboration, for the generation of "fundamentally new psychic experiences."³ "[I]n Bollas's model," Adam Phillips observes, "the aim is not so much understanding – finding out which character you are – but a freeing of the potentially endless process of mutual invention and reinvention.... It is a psychoanalysis committed ... not [to] truth, except in its most provisional sense, but possibility."⁴

In the ordinary understanding of the relationship between psychoanalysis and literature, the reader is in the position of the analyst and the writer is in the position of the patient. Bollas' model makes it possible to flip that understanding on its head. The analyst who supplies material for the patient to work on and move through is like a writer; the patient who works on and moves through that material is like a reader. "The psychoanalyst's creativity is essential to the patient's use of the analytic process," Bollas writes. "When the clinician puts a new idea to a patient, this mental object may open inner spaces for experiencing and knowing. The analytic object is in this sense being used and then discarded as the patient moves through the comment to another idea."⁵ The aim is not to get anywhere in particular, but to allow for the unfolding, over time, of the patient's distinctive way of creatively using whatever is most evocative to him or her. Ideally, Bollas writes, "[t]he patient uses elements of my personality fleetingly, for specific momentary use, in order to forge self from experience. I feel one use of me is succeeded by another, in a movement of uses, without this psychical dialectics forming itself into a story."⁶ "When this is taking place," he adds, "the feeling I often have is one of pleasure at being made use of and being useful. I also feel this way when I am with my children, or as a university professor when a student seeks me out for intensive discussion of an idea he is working on."⁷

The analogy I am suggesting here – writer is to analyst as reader is to patient – is one that I am mostly extrapolating from Bollas' work (and the analogy is, obviously, inexact). Occasionally, however, Bollas suggests the analogy himself, and when he does, the writer to whom he most often refers is Melville. In *The Evocative Object World*, for instance, he describes Ishmael's encounter with the painting in the entryway of the Spouter-Inn as a metafictional modeling of the kind of encounter that Melville hopes that his readers will have with *Moby-Dick*. It is, Bollas writes, "a sly aside from Melville to his reader: read on, read what you will; make of this novel whatever occurs to you. Any encounter with any powerfully evocative object, suggests the author, forces us to think and think again."[8] The value of Melville, for Bollas, is that he invites, like a good-enough analyst, a movement of uses, that he is capable of stimulating in his readers the same kind of unwilled mental darting that the painting stimulates in Ishmael: "– It's the Black Sea in a midnight gale. – It's the unnatural combat of the four primal elements. – It's a blasted heath. – It's a Hyperborean winter scene. – It's the breaking-up of the icebound stream of Time." Each of the five dashes in the above passage indicates a state of mind in which something is *about to be made* of the painting, in which Ishmael is full-to-bursting with something unknowable in advance. By eliciting free association – or, as Bollas prefers to call it, "free thinking" – a writer/analyst can regenerate in a reader/patient a sense of being in unpredictable existential motion, a motion that is partially but obscurely self-directed, a motion that stimulates an interest not only in what one is about to encounter but in what one is about to make of it.[9]

I say "regenerate" because, as Bollas compellingly argues, all but the most unprovided-for among us periodically existed, early on, in environments that elicited our "internal transformational abilities," environments that are primarily associated with maternal care.[10] "[T]he infant experiences the mother as a process that transforms his internal and external environment" – as, in Bollas' terminology, a "transformational object" – and in a good-enough treatment, the patient likewise "unconsciously experiences the analyst as a generative transformational object."[11] "To understand how the analytic situation invites regression," he writes,

> let us remind ourselves of certain aspects of the analytic experience: lying on the couch, the physical sensations of being held by this physical object; physical proximity to the analyst and his

person; the relief and pleasure (even amidst pain) of the analyst's seemingly undivided attentiveness to our self; the wonderfully secure experience provided by the temporal dimensions (fifty *uninterrupted* minutes, five times a week, for as long as is felt necessary!); our "cot-like" experience of the objects within the analytic space as we gaze now and again at them, those enduringly familiar objects that come from "his" or "her" world; the intrinsic permission given to us to lapse into unselfconscious dreamlike states allowing us simply to feel our being, to find its formations in different experiences, and to report our self to the analyst, having discovered now and then a surprise from within.[12]

It would be ridiculous to claim that such experiences are identical with the experiences of very young children or readers. It would be no less ridiculous, however, to claim that there is *no* relationship between them, that there are no analogical leaps to be made from river-stone to river-stone. Bollas, for one, openly and intensely wishes to be used in something like the way in which the mother, or the "maternal environment," is used, as a means of "transform[ing] facts of life into psychical materials ... and ... support[ing] the rightful function of unconscious work."[13]

Not every writer (or analyst or teacher or parent or painter – the list goes on) wants to be used like this. But Melville clearly does. In the introduction to the "Extracts" that precede the opening chapter of *Moby-Dick*, Ishmael advises his reader not to "take the higgle-dy-piggledy whale statements, however authentic, in these extracts, for veritable gospel cetology.... [They] are solely valuable or entertaining, as affording a glancing bird's eye view of what has been promiscuously said, thought, fancied, and sung of Leviathan, by many nations and generations, including our own" (*MD*, 8). Anyone who tries to determine the internal logic of the eighty text-scraps that make up "Extracts" will inevitably be frustrated, either by their repetitiveness (whales are big!) or by their triviality ("Very like a whale" [10]) or by their seeming irrelevance to the subject ("If you make the least damn bit of noise ... I will send you to hell" [16]). The same may be said of "Cetology," in which Ishmael, after regretting the absence of a "popular comprehensive classification" of "the various species of whales," offers up his own "easy outline one for the present," in which whale-species are sorted by size, on the model of folio, octavo, and duodecimo books (116). At the end of the chapter, one of the longest in the novel, his wildly fanciful "cetological System stand[s] ... unfinished, even as the great Cathedral of Cologne was left, with the crane still standing upon the top of the uncompleted tower." This is, as far as he is concerned, a *good* thing. "God keep me from ever completing anything," he writes. "This whole book is but a draught – nay, but the draught of a draught. Oh, Time, Strength, Cash, and Patience!" (125). The aim of both the chapter and the book is not to convey an "ultimate generalizing purpose" (115), but to keep going past all of the points at which it is possible to stop, to keep veering away from all of the points at which the circle could conceivably be closed.

The value of circumventing the urge to complete things – of tolerating an uncertainty about how things are going to turn out – is that it generates more things to work on and move through. In "[some] of my free drawings," the psychoanalytic theorist Marion Milner writes in *On Not Being Able to Paint,*

> a scribble turned into a recognizable object too soon, as it were;
> the lines drawn would suggest some object and at once I would
> develop them to make it look like that object. It seemed almost
> as if, at these moments, one could not bear the chaos and uncer-
> tainty about what was emerging long enough, as if one had to
> turn the scribble into some recognizable whole when in fact the
> thought or mood seeking expression had not yet reached that
> stage. And the result was a sense of false certainty, a compulsive
> and deceptive sanity, a tyrannical victory of the common sense
> view which always sees objects as objects, but at the cost of
> something else which was seeking recognition, something more
> to do with imaginative than with common sense reality.[14]

The same holds true for thinking, Heinrich von Kleist suggests in "On the Gradual Fabrication of Thoughts While Speaking." When "I talk about [what I am working on] with my sister, who is working in the same room," Kleist writes,

> I suddenly realize things that hours of brooding had perhaps been unable to yield.... [As long as] I do start with some sort of dark notion remotely related to what I am looking for, my mind, if it has set out boldly enough, being pressed to complete what it has begun, shapes that muddled idea into a form of new-minted clarity, even while my talking progresses, with the result that my full thought, to my astonishment, is completed with the period. I mumble inarticulately, drawl out my conjunctions, use unnecessary appositions, and avail myself of all other dilatory tricks to gain the time required for fabricating my idea in the workshop of Reason.[15]

For Milner and Kleist alike, the aim is not to maunder, visually or verbally, but to hold open, as long as possible, a space that is receptive to the incursion of what Milner describes, with respect to her patients, as "a force in them to do with growth, growth towards their own shape."[16] Writers, visual artists, thinkers, conversationalists – anyone making anything in which a "thought or mood seek[s] expression" – must "gain ... time" for themselves, use whatever "dilatory tricks" they have at their disposal, if they hope to be responsive to "something" in them that has "more to do with imaginative than with common sense reality."

So why does "Extracts" precede Chapter 1? Why is "Cetology" so silly? Why do some of the chapters take the form of scenes from a play? Why does Ishmael say, before describing what a bowl of chowder tastes like, "Oh sweet friends! Hearken to me" (67)? Why does he so often personify moods, feelings, and states of being ("Terrors upon terrors ran shouting through his soul" [52]; "The profoundest slumber slept upon him" [91]; "Ahab and anguish lay stretched together in one hammock" [156])? Why does he conjure up phrases like "blisteringly passed" (232), "slopingly projects" (234), "anticipatingly tossed" (234), "smackingly feasted" (236), and "slantingly ranged up" (279)? Why the rampageous verbal sham-battle in "The Advocate"? ("[W] halemen ... have no good blood in their veins." *"No good blood in their veins?"* "Good ... but then all confess that somehow whaling is not respectable." *"Whaling not respectable?"* "Oh, ... the whale himself has never figured in any grand imposing way." *"The whale never figured in any grand imposing way?"* [100]) Why do so many of the sentences, paragraphs, and chapters seem to have been written in order to find out what would be said in them? And why does it seem so hard for Ishmael to stop himself once he has gotten going? ("Nor is this all"; "This ... reminds me of another thing"; "A word or two more concerning this matter" [246]). The answer to all of the above questions is – to return to Bollas' argument about the analyst's function – that Melville wrote *Moby-Dick* "not to get anywhere in particular, but to allow for the unfolding, over time, of the [reader's] distinctive way of creatively using whatever is most evocative to him or her." If the reader does indeed "make of this novel whatever occurs to [him or her]," if one use of the novel is indeed "succeeded by another, in a movement of uses, without this psychical dialectics forming itself into a story," something vital will have happened, and it will have happened at least in part because Melville has, far more than most writers, opened himself up to the reader's successive uses of him.[17]

"Perverse as this may sound," the critic Elizabeth Savage writes,

> I believe *Moby-Dick* is an inclusive, even a feminist text....
> Its writing really requires a different reading practice, one that
> surrenders to its impossible abundance and honors its purposeful
> uncertainty, as well as its disruptions of narrative structure, like
> those distinguishing "plot" from "digression."... [M]y approach to
> *Moby-Dick* encourages students ... to live with the book, which
> after all is hardly plot driven, over a long period of time so that
> they are conscious of the ways their personal lives, their other
> classes and other forms of work, and the other texts in the course

participate in their reading process and are constantly building and remodeling their understanding as they get to know the book. In short, I teach the book not so students will see that it transcends time and differences but so that they will see that it includes them.[18]

What Savage inspiringly invites her students and readers to do is to treat *Moby-Dick* as an "evocative object," an occasion for their own discoveries of the ways in which they are "constantly building and remodeling their understanding as they get to know the book." When psychoanalysis is working, Bollas writes, when the analyst is providing "a place and a process that sanctions the inner movement of self states," when "time is allowed to move on, and then move on, and then move on," the patient begins to sense in himself or herself a "unique forming intelligence" that "works upon the stuff of life."[19] When *Moby-Dick* is working, when the reader is making an active, imaginative, non-narrative use of it, it can, as Savage suggests, interblend with the reader's active, imaginative, non-narrative uses of other aspects of existence. It can stimulate what Bollas describes as "the unconscious freedom necessary for creative living"; it can suspend, to some degree, the "anguished repetitions that terminate the dissemination of the self."[20]

Take, for instance, the following passage, which comes at the end of Ishmael's description of sitting in a whaleboat amidst "reposing whales" – some of them nursing newborns, others of them having sex – while, all about them, "outer concentric circles" of panicked whales are "swiftly going round and round":

> And thus, though surrounded by circle upon circle of consternations and affrights, did these inscrutable creatures at the centre freely and fearlessly indulge in all peaceful concernments; yea, serenely revelled in dalliance and delight. But even so, amid the tornadoed Atlantic of my being, do I myself still for ever centrally disport in mute calm; and while ponderous planets of unwaning woe revolve round me, deep down and deep inland there I still bathe me in eternal mildness of joy. (302–3)

"And thus," like "all this" and "all these," gathers the descriptions that have preceded it into a concentrated point of departure. Unlike those other phrases, however, it is oriented toward a concept-to-come; it leads to a simplified retracing of what Ishmael has just sketched – at the circumference, revolving circles of anxiety and fear; at the center, peaceful pleasures – which leads, in turn, to an analogy: like the whales at the center of the circle, Ishmael is calm and joyful in the midst of woe. But as the relative staleness of that summary should suggest, the conceptual take-away is less important to Ishmael than the reciprocally intensifying energies that the analogy unleashes. One of the most important things that the summary leaves out is the affective dimension of Ishmael's state of being, a dimension conveyed first by the antithetically charged yet rhetorically balanced "tornadoed Atlantic" and "mute calm," and then by the similarly wrenched-apart yet counterpoised "ponderous planets of unwaning woe" and "eternal mildness of joy." But it also leaves out the richly objectless verb "disport" (OF. dis- + porter, get carried away, seek amusement, enjoy oneself), which picks up sensual connotations from "indulge" and "revelled" in the previous sentence and whose impact is heightened by the clause's unpunctuated build-up to it ("do I myself still for ever centrally"). At the core of the conflictually structured self, Ishmael indicates, is a mute disporting, a calm, polymorphic frolicsomeness, an orientation toward treating oneself and one's existence as things with which one plays.

This is, of course, just one way of using that passage, of moving in and through it, of discovering the import, for oneself, of its patterns and stresses. I will end this chapter with another. Several years ago, a new acquaintance told me, after learning that I worked on Melville, that she had a story for me. A couple of decades earlier, her husband, a filmmaker, was dying of cancer in a hospital in Chicago. For several days he had been either unconscious or non-communicative. One day, just before he died, my acquaintance arrived in the hospital room and asked the nurse if he had said anything. The nurse said that he had been mumbling but that when she went to listen, it had turned out to be nonsense. Soon he began mumbling again. My acquaintance put her head close to his. This is what he was saying: "But even so, amid the tornadoed Atlantic of my being, do I myself still for ever centrally disport in mute calm; and while ponderous planets of unwaning woe revolve round me, deep down and deep inland there I still bathe me in eternal mildness of joy." It was the last thing that she ever heard him say.

6 A New Way of Being Happy

I saw the gooseflesh on my skin. I did not know what made it. I was not cold. Had a ghost passed over? No, it was the poetry. A spark flew off [Matthew] Arnold and shook me, like a chill. I wanted to cry; I felt very odd. I had fallen into a new way of being happy.

—Sylvia Plath

[The words of poets and philosophers] are ... blazes made by the axe of the human intellect on the trees of the otherwise trackless forest of human experience. They give you somewhere to go from.

—William James

The immediate invitation of Melville's writing, I have been arguing, is to make use of it in a free, moment-to-moment, forward-moving way. Over time, however, as my acquaintance's story should suggest, fragments of his texts can become accompaniers of one's life. One's overall experience of Melville can, moreover, take on a relatively lasting shape. In Bollas's case, working on *Moby-Dick* in graduate school enabled him to "move elements of [his] idiom into collaboration with the text and hence into being."[1] Now, as a result, whenever he thinks of *Moby-Dick*, he experiences "a kind of gathering of internal objects," a marshaling of "inner presences that are ... not intelligible, or even clearly knowable: just intense ghosts who ... inhabit the human mind." The "sustained inner form" of those presences, the long-term effect of his experiences with *Moby-Dick*, is, in his terminology, a genera, a dynamic structuring of "highly condensed psychic textures" that gives rise to a specific mode of creative activity.[2] The value of *Moby-Dick* – and of Melville in general, and of anything else that is capable of producing psychic textures of this kind – is not just that it can solicit a series of self-elaborations, but that it can grow, over time, into a generative internal object: something to turn to, somewhere to go from.

An illustration from another writer's work may be useful at this point. In "Long-Legged Fly," William Butler Yeats introduces us in the first stanza to Julius Caesar, "in the tent/Where the maps are spread,/His eyes fixed upon nothing,/A hand under his head"; in the second stanza to Helen of Troy, "her feet/Practic[ing] a tinker shuffle/ Picked up on a street"; and in the third and final stanza to Michael Angelo, "on that scaffolding," his "hand mov[ing] to and fro." Each stanza ends with an italicized couplet: *"Like a long-legged fly upon the stream/His mind"* – or, in Helen's case, *"Her mind"* – *"moves upon silence."*[3] "[P]ure concentration," the critic Charles Altieri observes, leads each of the three characters in the poem "beyond the cognitive functions of consciousness to some fundamental reality knowable only to the degree that one can feel its constitutive force."[4] "The refrain," Altieri goes on to say,

> is the poem's means of acknowledging that force and of seeking identification with it. For it not only points to the silence but also offers a mode of circling back on one's own states so that one might be able to glimpse what evades all our practical orientations. And this circling with increasing intensity is the best response lyric can offer to the history that always threatens to reduce it to irrelevance.[5]

The minor, quiet movements of all consciousnesses, not just famous ones, seek, when intensified by concentration, to coincide with a force that operates, indifferently, in the water-steppings of long-legged flies, Caesar's preparations for battle, Helen's picked-up dance, and Michael Angelo's to-and-fro brush-strokes. Although the stature of Caesar, Helen, and Michael Angelo can make them seem unapproachable, they are what they are only by virtue of their ability to give themselves over to a creative process in which anyone can participate. We can all develop, by means of that process, self-states with idiosyncratic orientations toward the world, and we can all, like Caesar, Helen, and Michael Angelo, seek, find, and make use of them. And the more that we make use of them – the more that we sing certain refrains – the more generative they can become.

If the first-stage value of Melville is that he makes himself available for use after use after use, the second-stage value is that those uses can contribute, over time, to the growth of a distinctive psychic potential. Every long-time reader of Melville will of course have a different set of responses upon hearing his name spoken or seeing one of his books; what matters most, in the present context, is that such response-sets exist, that they can be activated, and that they can be, once activated, a resource for living. If internal objects – intense ghosts – are evoked in one by the name of "Herman Melville," one can circle back on them, circle with increasing intensity, and evolve from them various means of keeping one's idiom in motion.

The process I have in mind here is very different from the process of storing and retrieving the gist of wisdom-statements. My acquaintance's husband memorized the specific form of Melville's sentence so that he could move through it as a thing separate from him, shifting from the rhythms of his own utterances to the rhythms of Melville's utterances, from his own tensions and terms to Melville's tensions and terms – and yet (I imagine) experiencing its form as a familiar separateness, one that he had paradoxically made his own by leaving it, lovingly, as it was. The sentence must have "spoken" to him, must have prompted his own intellectual and imaginative uses of it, his own rephrasings and applications, but it must also, like D. W. Winnicott's good-enough mother, have survived those creative destructions with its otherness intact. His memorization of the sentence might be thought of as an expression of gratitude, even joy. "You have value for me because of your survival of my destruction of you," Winnicott imagines the baby/subject saying to the mother/object. "From this moment," Winnicott writes, "the object is *in fantasy* always being destroyed. This quality of 'always being destroyed' makes the reality of the surviving object felt as such, strengthens the feeling tone, and contributes to object constancy. The object can now be used."[6]

The mother, in Winnicott's model, manifests her survival by "not retaliat[ing]."[7] The textual object manifests its survival by not being used up, by bouncing back, in a sense, from the reader's creative destruction of it. Toward the end of the dinner party in Virginia

Woolf's *To the Lighthouse*, Mrs. Ramsay hears her husband speaking. "He was repeating something," Woolf writes,

> and she knew it was poetry from the rhythm and the ring of exultation, and melancholy in his voice:
> *Come out and climb the garden path, Luriana Lurilee.*
> *The China rose is all abloom and buzzing with the yellow bee.*
> The words (she was looking at the window) sounded as if they were floating like flowers on water out there, cut off from them all, as if no one had said them, but they had come into existence of themselves.
> "And all the lives we ever lived and all the lives to be are full of trees and changing leaves." She did not know what they meant, but, like music, the words seemed to be spoken by her own voice, outside her self, saying quite easily and naturally what had been in her mind the whole evening while she said different things.[8]

The value to Mrs. Ramsay of the lines that her husband has memorized derives neither from their cultural status – they are from a then-unpublished poem by a Victorian lawyer – nor from their meaning. It derives, instead, from their resilient, resonant otherness. The words seem both to have "come into existence of themselves" and to be "spoken by her own voice"; they are "cut off from them all, as if no one had said them," and are also "saying quite easily and naturally what had been in her mind the whole evening." Like the branches of the elm trees outside the window, which she sees as she walks upstairs after dinner, they "help her stabilize her position. Her world was changing: they were still.... [She] insensibly approve[d] of the dignity of the trees' stillness, and now again of the superb upward rise (like the beak of a ship up a wave) of the elm branches as the wind raised them."[9]

Consider, in this context, the following passage from "The Pacific":

> There is, one knows not what sweet mystery about this sea, whose gently awful stirrings seem to speak of some hidden soul

beneath; like those fabled undulations of the Ephesian sod over
the buried Evangelist St. John. And meet it is, that over these
sea-pastures, wide-rolling watery prairies and Potters' Fields of
all four continents, the waves should rise and fall, and ebb and
flow unceasingly; for here, millions of mixed shades and shadows,
drowned dreams, somnambulisms, reveries; all that we call lives
and souls, lie dreaming, dreaming, still; tossing like slumberers
in their beds; the ever-rolling waves but made so by their restlessness. (*MD*, 367)

Who speaks in this passage? Not exactly the Ishmael to whom we
are introduced in the opening chapters of the novel – the brusque,
garrulous, occasionally hysterical, comfort-loving, Queequeg-loving
sailor on the whaleship *Pequod* – and not exactly "Herman Melville"
either. It is more like a "what" that speaks here, I think, a part of
Melville's consciousness finding its way, via a hypnotic aural pat-
terning and an openness to unconscious associations, to a vision
of the voluminousness and mysteriousness of the ocean depths. A
relatively straightforward imaginative foray ("There is, one knows
not what sweet mystery about this sea, whose gently awful stir-
rings seem to speak of some hidden soul beneath") is expanded by
the evocativeness of a simile ("like those fabled undulations of the
Ephesian sod over the buried Evangelist St. John") and then explodes
into an unsheltered mysticism. Why do the waves of the Pacific "rise
and fall, and ebb and flow unceasingly"? Because, astonishingly,
"here, millions of mixed shades and shadows, drowned dreams, somnambulisms, reveries; all that we call lives and souls, lie dreaming,
dreaming, still; tossing like slumberers in their beds; the ever-rolling
waves but made so by their restlessness." "Set against this image,"
the critic Warner Berthoff writes, "the career of an Ahab cannot make
any finally pre-emptive claim on our concern; and we might well say
that in such a passage *Moby-Dick* turns away from the design of tragedy."[10] Beyond and beneath tragedy's individualistic design, we – "all
that we call lives and souls" – exist amidst, and occasionally write or
speak from, the rhythms of a ceaseless unconscious processing.

What is most crucial in such passages is the hypnotic intensity of the attention, the near-ruthless living of the experience. Here is a related example, from "The Castaway":

> The sea had jeeringly kept his finite body up, but drowned the infinite of his soul. Not drowned entirely, though. Rather carried down alive to wondrous depths, where strange shapes of the unwarped primal world glided to and fro before his passive eyes; and the miser-merman, Wisdom, revealed his hoarded heaps; and among the joyous, heartless, ever-juvenile eternities, Pip saw the multitudinous, God-omnipresent, coral insects, that out of the firmament of waters heaved the colossal orbs. He saw God's foot upon the treadle of the loom, and spoke it; and therefore his shipmates called him mad. So man's insanity is heaven's sense; and wandering from all mortal reason, man comes at last to that celestial thought, which, to reason, is absurd and frantic; and weal or woe, feels then uncompromised, indifferent as his God. (321–2)

Again, what speaks here is the topic-riveted attentiveness that Melville was so capable of drawing on at this point in his career. Where is Pip's body? Afloat. Where is Pip's soul? Drowned – and yet not drowned (and now "the creative" kicks into gear), but alive and deep, in a place where, in a virtually unparaphrasable passage, "strange shapes of the unwarped primal world glided to and fro before his passive eyes; and the miser-merman, Wisdom, revealed his hoarded heaps." Part of the point of the passage, clearly, is to communicate to us a Truth – that a godless infinity of microforces assembles and disassembles every form of existence – that Pip's shipmates cannot or will not take in. Another part of the point, however, is to invite us to descend into something like the state of absorption out of which the passage was written, to accept, as Bollas puts it in a passage I quoted earlier on the nature of the analytic experience, the "permission given to us to lapse into unselfconscious dreamlike states allowing us simply to feel our being, to find its formations in different experiences, and to ... [discover] now and then a surprise from within."

That invitation is issued, in part, by something that we might think of as the *Moby-Dick* music.[11] Both the ending of the passage from "The Pacific":

> here, millions of mixed shades and shadows,
> drowned dreams, somnambulisms, reveries;
> all that we call lives and souls, lie dreaming,
> dreaming, still; tossing like slumberers in
> their beds; the ever-rolling waves but made
> so by their restlessness.

and the ending of the passage from "The Castaway":

> So man's insanity is heaven's sense;
> and wandering from all mortal reason,
> man comes at last to that celestial thought,
> which, to reason, is absurd and frantic;
> and weal or woe, feels then uncompromised,
> indifferent as his God.

fall, like so many other passages in *Moby-Dick*, into the rhythm of blank verse. In a well-known reading of *Moby-Dick*, the critic F. O. Matthiessen chastises Melville for his susceptibility to such rhythms. After reproducing in stanzaic form some examples of Shakespeare-like blank verse from "The Quarter-Deck," Matthiessen declares that "[t]he danger of such unconsciously compelled verse is always evident. As it wavers and breaks down again into ejaculatory prose, it seems never to have belonged to the speaker, to have been at best a ventriloquist's trick."[12] Something belonging neither to a character nor to the narrator nor to the author speaks out at such moments, Matthiessen argues, something that "distracts attention to itself" and thereby interferes with the development of a "greater whole."[13] But it is precisely this quality, this sense of words "floating like flowers

on water ... as if ... they had come into existence of themselves,"
that Melville seems to be seeking in such passages. *Moby-Dick* is
supposed to sound, at times, as though its writing has been "unconsciously compelled."[14]

The rhythm of blank verse is, moreover, only one of the many
ways in which Melville creates, in *Moby-Dick*, the effect of speech
that "seems never to have belonged to the speaker." One can hear in
several of its anaphoric runs, for example, an anonymous-seeming
incantatoriness:

> *Often, when* forced from his hammock by exhausting and intoler-
> ably vivid dreams of the night, which, resuming his own intense
> thoughts through the day, carried them on amid a clashing of
> phrensies, and whirled them round and round and round in his
> blazing brain, till the very throbbing of his life-spot became insuf-
> ferable anguish;
>
>   *and when*, as was sometimes the case, these spiritual throes in
> him heaved his being up from its base, and a chasm seemed open-
> ing in him, from which forked flames and lightnings shot up, and
> accursed fiends beckoned him to leap down among them;
>
>   *when* this hell in himself yawned beneath him, a wild cry
> would be heard through the ship; and with glaring eyes Ahab
> would burst from his stateroom, as though escaping from a bed
> that was on fire. (169)

As they narrated to each other their unholy adventures, their tales
of terror told in words of mirth;

   as their uncivilized laughter forked upwards out of them, like
the flames from the furnace;

   as to and fro, in their front, the harpooneers wildly gesticulated
with their huge pronged forks and dippers;

   as the wind howled on, and the sea leaped, and the ship groaned
and dived, and yet steadfastly shot her red hell further and further into the blackness of the sea and the night, and scornfully
champed the white bone in her mouth, and viciously spat round
her on all sides;

then the rushing Pequod, freighted with savages, and laden with fire, and burning a corpse, and plunging into that blackness of darkness, seemed the material counterpart of her monomaniac commander's soul. (327)

And now that at the proper time and place, after so long and wide a preliminary cruise, Ahab, – all other whaling waters swept – seemed to have chased his foe into an ocean-fold, to slay him the more securely there;

now, that he found himself hard by the very latitude and longitude where his tormenting wound had been inflicted; now that a vessel had been spoken which on the very day preceding had actually encountered Moby Dick; –

and now that all his successive meetings with various ships contrastingly concurred to show the demoniac indifference with which the white whale tore his hunters, whether sinning or sinned against;

now it was that there lurked a something in the old man's eyes, which it was hardly sufferable for feeble souls to see. (400)

Even though all three of these sentences play a meaningful role in the narrative, their composition seems to have been motivated, for the most part, by non-semantic concerns, by a desire to follow the strange lead of sonority and recursiveness. They evoke, in Altieri's words, "the imagination's capacity to dwell in intensive states that reach well beyond domains where the ego can assume any control." Deep within such sentences, one moves upon silence, approaching a "fundamental reality knowable only to the degree that one can feel its constitutive force" – a reality that gives rise, successively, to Ahab's "wild cry," the crew's "uncivilized laughter," and the "something" in Ahab's eyes.

"Reading Darwin," Elizabeth Bishop writes,

one admires the beautiful solid case being built up out of his endless, heroic observations ... and then comes a sudden relaxation, a forgetful phrase, and one feels the strangeness of his undertaking, sees the lonely young man, his eyes fixed on facts and minute details, sinking or sliding giddily off into the unknown. What one seems to want in art, in experiencing it, is the same thing that is necessary for its creation, a self-forgetful, perfectly useless concentration.[15]

One of the most important things that Melville offers us – and one of the easiest things to overlook – is a generous supply of moments at which we can feel "the strangeness of his undertaking," see him "sinking or sliding giddily off into the unknown." At such moments, moments when his "beautiful solid case" and "endless, heroic observations" dissolve into the strangeness of a self-forgetful concentration, he both opens himself to our successive uses of him and indicates that he can survive those uses. When he writes out of an unconsciously enriched concentration, as he so often does, he can call our own unconsciously enriched concentrations into action, freeing us up to use him as we will. But he can also generate, in such states, ways of putting things that make readers want not only to use them, but also to leave them, in the end, just as they found them. "Life stand still here," the painter Lily Briscoe imagines Mrs. Ramsay saying to herself after she has succeeded, through the force of her presence, in "making of the moment something permanent." "In the midst of chaos there was shape," Lily thinks. "[T]his eternal passing and flowing (she looked at the clouds going and the leaves shaking) was struck into stability. Life stand still here, Mrs. Ramsay said. 'Mrs. Ramsay! Mrs. Ramsay!' she repeated. She owed it all to her."[16]

7 The Meaning of *Moby-Dick*

I have been suggesting that Melville, for all of his masculinism, is capable of functioning as a maternal environment – as, in Bollas's terminology, a "transformational object." Part of what is made available to one when one feels the strangeness of Melville's undertaking is a sense of being near to estrangeability as such, to that which makes it possible for anything at all to be, as Melville puts it in *Clarel*, "differenced."[1] The joy of the good-enough maternal environment, is, similarly, the joy of being placed "under the deep spell of the uncanny," of being free to roam in a space whose defining features are "unintrusiveness, 'holding,' 'provision,' insistence on a kind of symbiotic or telepathic knowing, and facilitation from thought to thought or from affect to thought."[2] The memory of that environment does not disappear from consciousness with the advent of the transitional-object period or at any subsequent developmental stage. We are in fact, Bollas writes, continually engaged in "a wide-ranging collective search for an object that is identified with the metamorphosis of the self," an object that enables us "to remember not cognitively but existentially – through intense affective experience – a relationship which was identified with cumulative transformational experiences."[3]

When one feels a "deep subjective rapport" with such an object, the "anticipation of being transformed" can inspire one, Bollas suggests, "with a reverential attitude towards it."[4] This is, I think, why readers who develop a rapport with *Moby-Dick* tend to have not only an anticipatory interest in where it might take them but an at least quasi-reverential interest in where it comes from, why it was written, what it is "about." As I have already suggested, if we are too exclusively concerned with an artwork's meaning, we miss out on the full range of the experiences that it can offer. It would be foolish, however, to deny the existence of such concerns, to imagine that it is possible to police one's consciousness so effectively that no thoughts about the artwork's meaning could ever sneak their way in. Accordingly, in the spirit of Ishmael standing before the painting in the Spouter-Inn with interpretive ideas darting him through, and as another example of the uses to which *Moby-Dick* may be put, I will throw out, in this chapter, some thoughts on the meaning of *Moby-Dick*, thoughts that will, I hope, enable us to circle back, with an increased intensity, to the subject of maternality.

In "The Chase – First Day," after Moby Dick has finally appeared, "at every roll of the sea revealing his high sparkling hump," and after his hunters in their whaleboats have rowed close enough to see "the glistening white shadow from his broad, milky forehead" and the birds taking turns perching on a lance projecting from his hump, their "long tail feathers streaming like pennons," we are told that

> [o]n each soft side – coincident with the parted swell, that but
> once laving him, then flowed so wide away – on each bright side,
> the whale shed off enticings. No wonder there had been some
> among the hunters who, namelessly transported and allured by all
> this serenity, had ventured to assail it; but had fatally found that
> quietude but the vesture of tornadoes. Yet calm, enticing calm,
> oh, whale! thou glidest on, to all who for the first time eye thee,
> no matter how many in that same way thou may'st have bejug-
> gled and destroyed before. (409)

How could one's allegory-sensors not go off at this point? For the moment, at least, Melville seems to have, and to want his readers to have, a clear idea of the White Whale's meaning. That meaning is, moreover, almost startlingly simple. The whale is The World. To all who for the first time eye it, the whale/world is "calm, enticing calm," serenely transporting and alluring; on each soft, bright side, the whale/world "shed[s] off enticings." But the whale/world "bejuggle[s] and destroy[s]" all who actually encounter it, for it is not what it initially appears to be. Its "quietude [is] but the vesture of tornadoes." Just in case that isn't clear enough, Melville opens the next paragraph with a sentence that intensifies the allegorical imagery: "And thus, through the serene tranquilities of the tropical sea, among waves whose hand-clappings were suspended by exceeding rapture, Moby Dick moved on, still withholding from sight the full terrors of his submerged trunk, entirely hiding the wrenched hideousness of his jaw" (409).

This is by no means the first time in the novel that Melville has asked us to return to our memories of how enticing The World initially seemed and how tornadic it subsequently became. Here are a few of those earlier passages, with double back-slashes at the point where things turn traumatic:

> Though in many of its aspects this visible world seems formed in love, // the invisible spheres were formed in fright. (164)

> "The White Whale – the White Whale!" was the cry from captain, mates, and harpooneers ... while the dogged crew eyed askance, and with curses, the appalling beauty of the vast milky mass, that lit up by a horizontal spangling sun, shifted and glistened like a living opal in the blue morning sea.... // [O]f a sudden the boat struck as against a sunken ledge, and keeling over, spilled out the standing mate.... [T]he whale rushed round in a sudden mael-strom; seized the swimmer between his jaws; and rearing high up with him, plunged headlong again, and went down. (212)

> [F]ew thoughts of Pan stirred Ahab's brain, as standing like an iron statue at his accustomed place beside the mizen rigging, with one nostril he unthinkingly snuffed the sugary musk from the Bashee isles (in whose sweet woods mild lovers must be walking), // and with the other consciously inhaled the salt breath of the new found sea; that sea in which the hated White Whale must even then be swimming. (367–8)

> At such times, under an abated sun; afloat all day upon smooth, slow heaving swells; seated in his boat, light as a birch canoe; and so sociably mixing with the soft waves themselves, that like hearth-stone cats they purr against the gunwale; these are the

times of dreamy quietude, when beholding the tranquil beauty
and brilliancy of the ocean's skin, // one forgets the tiger heart
that pants beneath it; and would not willingly remember, that
this velvet paw but conceals a remorseless fang. (372)

"Oh, grassy glades! oh, ever vernal endless landscapes in the soul;
in ye, – though long parched by the dead drought of the earthy
life, – in ye, men yet may roll, like young horses in new morning
clover; and for some few fleeting moments, feel the cool dew of
the life immortal on them. Would to God these blessed calms
would last. // But the mingled, mingling threads of life are woven
by warp and woof: calms crossed by storms, a storm for every
calm." (373)

"[I]t is a mild, mild wind, and a mild looking sky; and the air
smells now, as if it blew from a far-away meadow; they have
been making hay somewhere under the slopes of the Andes,
Starbuck, and the mowers are sleeping among the new-mown hay.
// Sleeping? Aye, toil we how we may, we all sleep at last on the
field. Sleep? Aye, and rust amid greenness; as last year's scythes
flung down, and left at the half-cut swaths – Starbuck!" (407)

The problem with The World, as Melville thinks we all secretly
know, is that it seems formed in love – sugary, mild, dreamy, cool,
calm – but harbors within itself, for each of us, sources of fright.
The problem is not just that each of us makes unpleasant discoveries – that life is brief, for instance, or that joy is evanescent, or
that one's knowledge is partial, or that one's influence is slight, or
that one's experiences are limited, or that one's intimacies are either
hallucinatory or intermittent. Nor is it just that all such discoveries
come as shocks, as a result of the fact that The World is, to all who for
the first time eye it, so beautiful. It is, above all else, that they con-
tinue to come as shocks, because The World never stops being beautiful, never stops enticing us in ways that lead us to forget whatever we
have learned. Ahab doesn't go mad because the White Whale bites off

his leg; he goes mad because he has to swim, in the aftermath of his dismemberment, "into the serene, exasperating sunlight, that smiled on, as if at a birth or a bridal" (156).

In the figure of Ahab, Melville externalizes the part of himself that is saddened and infuriated by the enticing/betraying structure of The World, in the hopes that at least some of his readers will feel spoken for, will feel their own sadness and fury flowing out. In "Dusk," after a "burst of revelry from the forecastle," Starbuck cries, "Hark! ... that revelry is forward! mark the unfaltering silence aft! Methinks it pictures life. Foremost through the sparkling sea shoots on the gay, embattled, bantering bow; but only to draw dark Ahab after it, where he broods within his sternward cabin, builded over the dead water of the wake, and further on, hunted by its wolfish gurgling" (144). Everyone, Starbuck suddenly feels, banters in public while brooding in private; everyone has a "dark Ahab" in his or her sternward cabin, permanently aware of the death over which The World is built and the wolfishness that is never far behind it; everyone experiences, at some time or other, the full traumatic force of The World's enticement and betrayal.

The central aim of the Ahab/Moby Dick story is to make us more aware of the parts of ourselves that have registered that shock, and, as a result, more aware of what we secretly have in common with each other. That can only happen, however, if we partially identify with Ahab and partially share his perception of Moby Dick. It is worth considering, in this context, the allegorical thrust of "The Spirit-Spout." "[O]ne serene and moonlight night," Ishmael tells us,

> when all the waves rolled by like scrolls of silver; and, by their
> soft, suffusing seethings, made what seemed a silvery silence,
> not a solitude; on such a silent night a silvery jet was seen far
> in advance of the white bubbles at the bow.... [When Fedallah's]
> unearthly voice was heard announcing that silvery, moon-lit jet,
> every reclining mariner started to his feet as if some winged spirit
> had lighted in the rigging, and hailed the mortal crew. "There she
> blows!" Had the trump of judgment blown, they could not have
> quivered more; yet still they felt no terror; rather pleasure.... But

> though the ship ... swiftly sped, and though from every eye, like
> arrows, the eager glances shot, yet the silvery jet was no more
> seen that night. Every sailor swore he saw it once, but not a sec-
> ond time. (192)

Every few nights, the spirit-spout appears, is chased, and then "disappear[s] as if it had never been" (193). The quivering pleasure that
Ishmael and his shipmates initially feel gives way to a superstitious
dread that the "unnearable spout was cast by [Moby Dick]" and that it
is "treacherously beckoning [them] on and on" with its "calm, snow-
white, and unvarying ... fountain of feathers" (193, 194). Not only
to Ahab, but also to each of the sailors on the *Pequod*, the feathery
spout, the signifier of calmness and pleasure, appearing once and then
vanishing, induces pleasure crossed with dread. *Once the world filled
me with pleasure; then it became a source of fright; now, under the
spell of Ahab, I seek to annihilate the pleasure and the fright alike.*

"[A]ll these chapters might be naught," Ishmael writes in the
"The Whiteness of the Whale," if he cannot communicate to us, even
if only "in some dim, random way," how excruciating it is to be in
relation to something that evokes such intense sensations of pleasure and fright – how excruciating it is, in other words, to exist, to
be in relation to The World (159). And if all these chapters are indeed
for naught, if he cannot get through to us, then that condition will
become virtually impossible for him to bear. Few things are worse,
he informs us in "Loomings," than feeling alone in one's experiencing of those sensations, than walking down streets where everyone
else seems unaware, and likely to remain unaware, of what you are
experiencing, in spite of the fact that they are in the same existential
position that you are. It is the kind of thing that can make you feel
like "methodically knocking people's hats off" (18), that can make
going to sea, where your existential position is quite clear, preferable
to remaining on land. It can also make you feel like writing what
Melville describes, in a letter to Hawthorne, as "a wicked book" – a
book that knocks its readers' hats off, takes them down a notch – and
yet feel "spotless as the lamb" about it, insofar as the book's aim is to
reveal our shared existential position, to indicate that no one is alone

(*C*, 212). It can make you try, in your book's first chapter, to draw out your readers' already-existing knowledge of pleasure/fright – to suggest that "[i]f they but knew it, almost all men in their degree, some time or other, cherish very nearly the same feelings towards the ocean with me" (*MD*, 18) – and then to identify the attraction to water with an attraction to a reality that we all knew before we knew much of anything, the reality of a "tormenting, mild image" (20), inseparable from one's self, that appeared and disappeared, over and over again. "It is the image of the ungraspable phantom of life," Ishmael tells us, "and this is the key to it all" (20).

In Toni Morrison's *Beloved*, when Paul D follows Sethe into her house, he walks "smack into a pool of pulsing red light" and "a wave of grief soak[s] him."[5] This place of grief, where "a kind of weeping clung to the air," is, Sethe tells him, the ghost of her third child.[6] Over the course of Morrison's novel, the experience of being in that space, of touching and being touched by a ghost – the ghost of the third child and of every other beloved black person killed as a result of slavery and racism – both undoes and restores Paul D. "She reminds me of something," he tells Sethe in one of their final conversations. "Something, look like, I'm supposed to remember."[7] Something similar may be said of Ahab and all of the parts of the other characters and of Ishmael/Melville that coincide with him; they are, or can be, a means of access to someplace important in oneself – not necessarily to the psychic residues of what was loved amidst and destroyed by slavery and racism, obviously, but certainly to, in Morrison's words, "some ocean-deep place" that one "once belonged to," a place that potentially incorporates such residues, as it clearly does for Pip.[8] Only if it is possible to identify a part of ourselves with Ahab, a part of ourselves that is capable of feeling "the sum of all the general rage and hate felt by [the] whole race from Adam down" (*MD*, 156), is it possible to become deeply interested in the effects of those feelings. What, if anything, will survive Ahab's destructiveness? What will remain when the action of Ahab's drama is complete?

The most important answer to those questions, I think, is that The World survives Ahab's assault on it, both allegorically (the whale lives on) and actually. It is hard to feel good about that fact right after the *Pequod* goes down, when the ocean's surface is likened to a "great shroud," a signifier and anonymizer of death, "roll[ing] on as it rolled five thousand years ago" (427). At this moment, as at many earlier moments in the book, the ongoingness of the world can seem terrifying in its stolidity, its unresponsiveness to human concerns. But then, in the epilogue, as a result of the same implacable laws that govern the waves' movements, the lifebuoy/coffin uprises and breaches the ocean's surface, giving Ishmael something to hang on to until the *Rachel* arrives. Accidentally, "without premeditated reference to this world or the next" (357), Ishmael survives. The whale swims away. The world – which is, as it turns out, capable of bearing our psychic investments in it – spins on.

And that means that we are free to keep unconsciously working on and playing with the world. The value of the meaning of *Moby-Dick* that I am offering up here is that it gives us, to return to William James's phrase, somewhere to go from. We can *use* this understanding of the world's usability. Like a child who does not fear retaliation, who feels free to fantasize the mother out of actuality and into psychic existence, we can transfigure at will, without ever losing or destroying the actual. The world comes back when we put the book down; the book comes back when we pick it up again. Only after one has discovered, as the result of an all-out experience of transformative use, that "the other is in some basic way outside one's boundaries," can one begin to experience, precisely "*because* there is radical otherness," a "new kind of freedom," a "new realness of self-feeling."[9] When Pierre first perceives the "hopeless gloom" of *Hamlet*'s "interior meaning" – that "all meditation is worthless, unless it prompt to action" – he "drop[s] the too true volume from his hand" and his "petrifying heart drop[s] hollowly within him." What Pierre does not realize, the narrator tells us, is that "Hamlet, though a thing of life, was, after all, but a thing of breath, evoked by the wanton magic of a creative hand, and as wantonly dismissed at last into endless halls of hell and night" (*P*, 169). Hamlet was creatively evoked in order to be creatively used, and then, once used, dismissed – which is to say that *Hamlet* is just as much about the joyous freedom of the creatively active mind as it is about the traumatically unsuturable gap between thinking and acting. "It is the not impartially bestowed privilege of the more final insights," *Pierre*'s narrator goes on to say, "that at the same moment they reveal the depths, they do, sometimes, also reveal – though by no means so distinctly – some answering heights" (*P*, 169).

8 As If!

I hear that he is now so engaged in a new work [*Moby-Dick*] as frequently not to leave his room till quite dark in the evening – when he for the first time during the whole day partakes of solid food – he must therefore write under a state of morbid excitement which will soon injure his health – I laughed at him somewhat and told him that the recluse life he was leading made his city friends think that he was slightly insane – he replied that long ago he had come to the same conclusion himself – but if he left home to look after Hungary the cause in hunger would suffer.

—Sarah Morewood

An exclamation point is entire Mardi's autobiography.

—Melville, *Mardi*

"Six months at sea!" Melville writes in the first sentence of *Typee*. That sentence gives rise to another exclamatory sentence: "Yes, reader, as I live, six months out of sight of land; cruising after the sperm-whale beneath the scorching sun of the Line, and tossed on the billows of the wide-rolling Pacific – the sky above, the sea around, and nothing else!" Thirteen more exclamations tumble out in the first seven paragraphs, marking distress ("Those glorious bunches of bananas which once decorated our stern and quarter-deck have, alas, disappeared! and the delicious oranges which hung suspended from our tops and stays – they, too, are gone!"), desire ("Oh! for a refreshing glimpse of one blade of grass – for a snuff at the fragrance of a handful of the loamy earth!"), dread-tinged delight ("The Marquesas!"), a world-animating sensibility ("Poor old ship!"), and a contagious buoyancy of spirit ("Hurra, my lads!") (*T*, 21–2). In each of these instances, and in a slew of similar ones in the works that follow – "Moby Dick bodily burst into view!", say, or "Ah, Bartleby!" or "God bless Captain Vere!" – Melville inflects an otherwise stable utterance with the unstable tonality of a brief cry. We are meant to hear, retroactively, a sudden heightening of force, a tonal quality that is both singular, in that it is elicited in a certain speaker by a certain occasion, and general, in that it emerges from a reservoir of vocal potential that is common to our species (and to many other species as well).

There are, of course, other ways of evoking that tonal quality in print; one can italicize certain words or phrases, for example, or use preliminary intensifiers like "just." After writing about a morning when "[t]he sun had come up brilliantly after a heavy rain, and the trees were glistening and very wet," and a young man had, "[o]n some impulse, plain exuberance, I suppose," jumped and caught a branch, causing "a storm of luminous water" to pour down on himself and the young woman with whom he was walking, John Ames, the narrator of Marilynne Robinson's *Gilead*, reflects on

> the care it costs me not to use certain words more than I ought to. I am thinking about the word "just." I almost wish I could have written that the sun just *shone* and the tree just *glistened*, and the water just *poured* out of it and the girl just *laughed* – when it's used that way it does indicate a stress on the word that follows it, and also a particular pitch of the voice. People talk that way when they want to call attention to a thing existing in excess of itself, so to speak, a sort of purity or lavishness, at any rate something ordinary in kind but exceptional in degree. So it seems to me at the moment. There is something real signified by that word "just" that proper language won't acknowledge.[1]

Throughout his career, but especially in its early phase, Melville frequently "talk[s] that way" – frequently "calls attention to a thing existing in excess of itself." In doing so, he contributes to what the critic Rosi Braidotti describes as an ethics of "generative vitality," which sets an "expansion, acceleration, or intensification of interrelation" against "a decrease, a dimming or slowing down, a dampening of intensity, which reduces the capacity for relations with others."[2] When one's quantity of feeling rises – when, in "The Spirit-Spout," the "strange, upheaving, lifting tendency of the taffrail breeze fill[s] the hollows" of the sails (192) – one's potential for interrelation goes up. When one's quantity of feeling falls – when, in "The Pequod Meets the Rachel," the sails "all [fall] together as blank bladders that are burst" (396) – one's potential for interrelation goes down.

One of the things that the reviewers of Melville's first books liked most about them was their generative vitality, their capacity to make the reader feel, as Evert Duyckinck puts it in a review of *Redburn*, as if he or she is being infused with "the force of a life current from the writer's own heart."[3] After an evening spent with Melville in 1849, the writer and literary hobnobber Nathaniel Parker Willis informed the readers of the *New York Home Journal* that "Herman Melville, with his cigar and his Spanish eyes, *talks* Typee and Omoo, just as you find the flow of his delightful mind on paper. Those who have only read his books know the man – those who have only seen the man have a fair idea of his books."[4] At that stage of his life, Melville seems to have enjoyed such performances – to have thought of himself as, in part, a galvanizer-at-large, bringing vitality, by way of "the flow of his delightful mind," to the devitalized. In the journal he kept during his 1849 trip to England, he describes his efforts to "create some amusement" during the voyage by mock-arraigning a friend "before the Captain on a criminal charge" and then "put[ting] the Captain in the Chair, & arguing the question, 'which was best, a monarchy or a republic?'"[5] In London, upon meeting the publisher Edward Moxon, he found him "at first very stiff, cold, clammy, & clumsy. Managed to bring him to, tho', by clever speeches" (*J*, 23). The exclamatory passages in his early books seem to have had, in his mind, a similarly restorative and relational dimension; by bringing his readers "to," they might bring his readers toward him, and then, through him, toward others. His aspiration in such passages is not to instruct and delight, and certainly not to offer a stay against confusion, but instead to plunge us into a stimulating psychic environment, so that we can, to paraphrase Zora Neale Hurston, utilize ourselves all over.[6]

Here are a few examples of the quality that I have in mind, taken from *Redburn*, *White-Jacket*, and *Moby-Dick*:

Come, Wellingborough, why not push on for London? – Hurra!
What say you? Let's have a peep at St. Paul's! Don't you want to
see the queen? Have you no longing to behold the duke? Think of
Westminster Abbey, and the Tunnel under the Thames! Think of
Hyde Park, and the ladies!

But then, thought I again, with my hands wildly groping in my
two vacuums of pockets – who's to pay the bill? (R, 245)

"Ah! barber, have you no heart? This beard has been caressed
by the snow-white hand of the lovely Tomasita of Tombez – the
Castilian belle of all Lower Peru. Think of *that*, barber! I have
worn it as an officer on the quarter-deck of a Peruvian man-of-
war. I have sported it at brilliant fandangoes in Lima. I have been
alow and aloft with it at sea. Yea, barber! it has streamed like an
Admiral's pennant at the mast-head of this same gallant frigate,
the Neversink! Oh! barber, barber! it stabs me to the heart! –
Talk not of hauling down your ensigns and standards when van-
quished – what is *that*, barber! to striking the flag that
Nature herself has nailed to the mast!"

Here noble Jack's feelings overcame him; he drooped from the
animated attitude into which his enthusiasm had momentarily
transported him; his proud head sunk upon his chest, and his
long, sad beard almost grazed the deck. (WJ, 360–1)

"Woe to him whom this world charms from Gospel duty! Woe to
him who seeks to pour oil upon the waters when God has brewed
them into a gale! Woe to him who seeks to please rather than to
appal! Woe to him whose good name is more to him than goodness! Woe to him who, in this world, courts not dishonor! Woe to
him who would not be true, even though to be false were salva-
tion! Yea, woe to him who, as the great Pilot Paul has it, while
preaching to others is himself a castaway!"

He drooped and fell away from himself for a moment; then lifting
his face to them again, showed a deep joy in his eyes. (MD, 53–4)

The passages are characteristically Melvillean not only in the sud-
denness and intensity of their animation but also in the evanescence
of that state. Redburn's happy anticipations ("Let's have a peep at
St. Paul's!") are broken in upon by the memory of his cashlessness;
Jack Chase, at the peak of his peroration, suddenly "droop[s] from the
animated attitude into which his enthusiasm had momentarily transported him"; Father Mapple, after reaching the climax of an anaphoric
extravaganza, similarly "droop[s] and [falls] away from himself for a
moment." A great many other writers have been aware that, in Poe's
words, "all intense excitements are, through a psychal necessity,
brief," but not many of them have dramatized that awareness as often
as Melville did.[7] Not many of them have been as struck, that is, by
the mere fact of our susceptibility to such elevations and descents.

Why does Melville find this fact so striking? In part, I think,
because it is so closely connected to his belief in what writing and
reading are for. As the markings and jottings in the margins of his
books abundantly indicate, he was an animated and animation-seek-
ing reader ("Bully for Emerson!"; "Alas! the fool again!"; "True &
admirable! Bravo!"; "Nothing can be truer or better said").[8] And as
one can infer both from the nature of his style and from his more
self-referential accounts of literary composition, writing often was,
for him, an impassioned and impassioning process. "[W]hat was it
that originally impelled Lombardo to the [writing of the Kostanza]?"
Babblanja rhetorically asks in *Mardi*. "Primus and forever, a full
heart: – brimful, bubbling, sparkling; and running over like the flagon
in your hand, my lord" (M, 592). When Ishmael writes, in the final
sentence of "The Decanter," "And this empties the decanter" (MD,
344), the implication is that he and/or the reader has at that moment
finished off a bottle of wine or liquor, that writing and/or reading
this chapter on gormandizing and fuddlement has been a stimulating and perhaps intoxicating experience. Likewise, when Melville
tells Sarah Morewood – as she reports in the letter that I quote from
in the epigraph to this chapter – that if he were to interrupt the writing of *Moby-Dick* to support the cause of Hungarian independence,
"the cause in hunger would suffer," the implication is less that he
has a family to feed than that writing *Moby-Dick* satisfies a hunger

in him and that reading *Moby-Dick* might satisfy a similar hunger in others. As when he promises Sophia Hawthorne that "[t]he next chalice I shall commend will be a rural bowl of milk," he conveys, in such instances, an understanding of writing as something that can sustain and stimulate, in the most basic of ways, writer and reader alike.

The larger reason why Melville so often dramatizes the oscillations of moods, however, is that he thinks that something crucial is left out of our conception of existence if we ignore or underplay them. "Oh, Charlie!" cries *The Confidence-Man*'s cosmopolitan, playing a loan-requesting friend named Frank, to Egbert, playing a loan-denying friend named Charlie, "you talk not to a god, a being who in himself holds his own estate, but to a man who, being a man, is the sport of fate's wind and wave, and who mounts towards heaven or sinks towards hell, as the billows roll him in trough or on crest" (*CM*, 243). Egbert/Charlie's cool response is that each of us can be, and therefore must be, strong enough to go it alone: "Tut! Frank. Man is no such poor devil as that comes to – no poor drifting sea-weed of the universe. Man has a soul; which, if he will, puts him beyond fortune's finger and the future's spite" (243). In a cultural environment in which self-reliance is strictly mandated for the struggling and casually imputed to the already-secure, it can be hard to get relatively comfortable people like Egbert to acknowledge that we mount and sink in response to forces beyond our control. "[I]n the inexorable and inhuman eye of mere undiluted reason," Melville writes in *Pierre*, "all grief, whether on our own account, or that of others, is the sheerest unreason and insanity" (*P*, 186). Knowing it may seem insane, Melville nevertheless tries, in many of his exclamatory passages, not only to raise spirits but to give voice to a culturally suppressed truth: that we are all at the mercy of fate's wind and wave, all liable to be rolled by the billows in troughs or on crests.[9]

Something similar may be said of another signature feature of his books: the similes that so plentifully burst forth in them. Those similes very often express, as his exclamations do, a generative vitality; they exist not so much to clarify a statement or description as to evoke its capacity to be related to other things – its capacity to be, imaginatively speaking, somewhere good to go from. Here, for instance, is White-Jacket's brief description of Staten Land, an uninhabited island twenty-nine miles off the southern tip of Argentina:

> On our starboard beam, *like a pile of glaciers in Switzerland,* lay this Staten Land, gleaming in snow-white barrenness and solitude. Unnumbered white albatross were skimming the sea near by, and clouds of smaller white wings fell through the air *like snowflakes.* High, towering in their own turbaned snows, the far-inland pinnacles loomed up, *like the border of some other world.* Flashing walls and crystal battlements, *like the diamond watch-towers along heaven's furthest frontier.* (*WJ,* 116; emphasis added)

It is strikingly different from the description of Staten Land in Richard Henry Dana, Jr.,'s *Two Years Before the Mast,* a book that Melville liked so much that it made him feel, as he told Dana in a letter, "welded to him":

> The land [that had been sighted] was the island of Staten Land, just to the eastward of Cape Horn; and a more desolate-looking spot I never wish to set eyes upon; – bare, broken, and girt with rocks and ice, with here and there, between the rocks and broken hillocks, a little stunted vegetation of shrubs. It was a place well suited to stand at the junction of the two oceans, beyond the reach of human cultivation, and encounter the blasts and snows of a perpetual winter.[10]

The four italicized similes in Melville's description turn the interaction between White-Jacket's consciousness and Staten Land into something much more than a reciprocation of bleaknesses. Instead of simply panning across the prominent features of the island, as Dana does, White-Jacket enriches those features, paralleling their gleaming with the gleaming of Swiss glaciers, picturing flocks of small white birds snowing down onto it, and finally investing the aspect of its mountains with an otherworldliness that inspires him to leap, in the passage's final, fragmentary sentence, all the way up to the glittering outposts of Heaven's empire. Staten Land may be uninhabitable – to this day, it has no permanent residents – but it is not, as Melville shows, "beyond the reach of human cultivation."

What is cultivated by the similes in such passages is, above all else, a sense of vitality. Emerging not from the requirements of characterization or plotting or theme, but from an essentially irrational willing of something rather than nothing, Melville's similes "take the side of life," as Seamus Heaney argues with respect to the other-than-functional elements of poetry, which is to say that they "[opt] for the condition of overlife."[11] "[N]ature is but a name for excess," William James writes. "[E]very point in her opens out and runs into the more." "In the pulse of inner life immediately present now in each of us," James goes on to say,

> is a little past, a little future, a little awareness of our own body, of each other's persons, of these sublimities we are trying to talk about, of the earth's geography and the direction of history, of truth and error, of good and bad, and of who knows how much more? Feeling, however dimly and subconsciously, all these things, your pulse of inner life is continuous with them, belongs to them and they to it.[12]

Profusely blossoming similes are often criticized, the critic Theo Davis observes, for their "lightness," their "intractably accessory nature," their "impertinence ... to meaning."[13] But in a world in which even the "smallest state of consciousness, concretely taken, overflows its own definition," in which there is no telling "how far into the rest of nature we may have to go in order to get entirely beyond its overflow," such similes might more accurately be seen as concatenating signs of life, stimulating indices of "the more."[14]

Consider, in this context, three passages from Melville's "Cock-a-Doodle-Doo! Or, The Crowing of the Noble Cock Beneventano" (1853), a story about a depressed man whose spirits are revived by the crowing of a rooster:

After an unwontedly sound, refreshing sleep I rose early, feeling
like a carriage-spring – light – elliptical – airy – buoyant *as stur-
geon-nose* – and, *like a foot-ball*, bounded up the hill.[15]

Hark! *Like a clarion!* Yea, *like a jolly bolt of thunder with bells
to it* – came the all-glorious and defiant crow! Ye gods, how it set
me up again! Right on my pins! Yea, verily on stilts! (110; emphasis added)

[I saw a] cock, more *like a golden eagle* than a cock. A cock, more
like a Field-Marshal than a cock. A cock, more *like Lord Nelson
with all his glittering arms on, standing on the Vanguard's
quarter-deck going into battle*, than a cock. A cock, more *like
the Emperor Charlemagne in his robes at Aix la Chapelle*, than a
cock.
    Such a cock!
    He was of a haughty size, stood haughtily on his haughty legs.
His colors were red, gold, and white. The red was on his crest
alone, which was a mighty and symmetric crest, *like unto Hector's
helmet, as delineated on antique shields.* His plumage was snowy,
traced with gold. He walked in front of the shanty, *like a peer of the
realm*; his crest lifted, his chest heaved out, his embroidered trap-
pings flashing in the light. His pace was wonderful. He looked *like
some noble foreigner.* He looked *like some Oriental king in some
magnificent Italian Opera.* (114; emphasis added)

The first thing that should be said about the similes in these passages
is that they arise from, and are meant to inspire in the reader, an
ultimately unsourceable exuberance. The title of the story refers us
not to the cock – one of the signifiers of the narrator's exuberance is
a fondness for phallic punning – but to a "Crowing" with a capital
"C," a mode of vocal expression that did not begin with and will
not end with the individual crower. (At the story's conclusion, the
cock, his owner, and his owner's family are dead, but the narrator
continues to "crow late and early with a continual crow": the story's

last line is "COCK-A-DOODLE-DOO! – OO! – OO! – OO! – OO!"
[120]) The narrator's redundant, extravagant, abounding similes tend
not to convey perceptual information very effectively. (What does "a
jolly bolt of thunder with bells to it" sound like? What do a golden
eagle, a Field-Marshal, Lord Nelson, and the Emperor Charlemagne
collectively look like?) What they tend to convey, instead, is the joy
of redescribability, the pleasurable awareness that there is, in the philosopher Graham Harman's words, "always something more to [an
object] than whatever we see or say."[16]

Only under certain circumstances, however, is that awareness
pleasurable. In "John Marr," an ex-sailor with a "void at heart," living in the Illinois town where his wife and child are buried, tries to
"fill that void by cultivating social relations" with his neighbors.[17]
But whenever the "lone-hearted mariner" sought

> to divert his own thoughts from sadness, and in some degree
> interest theirs, by adverting to aught removed from the crosses
> and trials of their personal surroundings, naturally enough he
> would slide into some marine story or picture, but would soon
> recoil upon himself and be silent, finding no encouragement to
> proceed. Upon one such occasion an elderly man – a blacksmith,
> and at Sunday gatherings an earnest exhorter – honestly said to
> him, "Friend, we know nothing of that here." (395)

The problem, as the narrator points out, is that if one is trying to
cultivate meaningful relations, "one cannot always be talking about
the present, much less speculating about the future; one must needs
recur to the past." And "the past of John Marr was not the past of
these pioneers," neither actually nor intellectually nor imaginatively. "So limited unavoidably was the mental reach, and by con-
sequence the range of sympathy, in this particular band of domestic
emigrants," the narrator writes, "that the ocean, but a hearsay to
their fathers, had now through yet deeper inland removal become
to themselves little more than a rumor traditional and vague" (394).
As a result, John Marr's awareness of "aught removed from ... their
personal surroundings" – "the free-and-easy tavern-clubs affording

cheap recreation of an evening in certain old and comfortable seaport towns of that time," for instance, or "the companionship afloat of the sailors of the same period" – has nowhere to go (395). Thrown "more and more upon retrospective musings," he consoles himself with memories of his former shipmates, memories that eventually become so vivid that the story vanishes into a poem in which he "striv[es] ... to get into verbal communion with them" (397).

What John Marr is most moved to do, in his attempted conversations with his neighbors, is to infuse the present with the past, to link a perception with something that it is like or unlike. ("'It is the bed of a dried-up sea,' said the companionless sailor – no geologist – to himself, musing at twilight upon the fixed undulations of that immense alluvial expanse bounded only by the horizon." [395–6]) Such movements of consciousness are, as the philosopher Elizabeth Grosz observes, the only means by which the present can become something other than an imprisoning orientation toward practical concerns. "[I]n order to act upon [an] object," Grosz writes, perception eliminates all of the "qualities, properties, and contexts" that are irrelevant to that action; memory, by contrast, "returns to objects the rich potential they have for functioning outside their familiar uses."[18] Even the simplest statement of a relation between perception and memory – the prairie is like the ocean – is capable of generating a "productive circuit" in which "each qualifies the other," thereby creating "the possibility of a reflective perception or a directed recollection."[19] But the "unresponsiveness" of John Marr's neighbors – an unresponsiveness that is, he feels, "of a piece with the apathy of Nature" – precludes the establishment of that circuit (395). By canceling the possibility of a relationship, it drives John Marr into spectral company, into the unrestful stasis of compulsive melancholic projections.

Against that backdrop, it is perhaps easier to see why Melville is so often drawn to similes. By self-consciously establishing relationships between objects, similes remind us that there is, as Babbalanja says in *Mardi*, "more to be thought of than to be seen" (*M*, 352) – more to objects and the subjective perception of objects than at first appears. In certain cases, as we have seen, that movement in the

direction of "the more" can feel painfully abyssal, like the beginning
of a descent into a raging Heraclitean flux. In the case of a simile,
however, it can feel like stepping from one object to another, each
of which continues to be, in Harman's words, a "unified entit[y]
with specific qualities that are autonomous from us and from each
other."[20] Because similes are less pretentious than metaphors and
symbols, because they express a desire to enhance the present with
the latent moreness of consciousness and objectivity, as opposed to
transcending and thereby redeeming it, they tend to be more oriented
than those other forms of figurative language toward simple, this-
worldly relations. "The nighthawk circled overhead in the sunny
afternoons," Thoreau writes in *Walden*,

> *like a mote in the eye, or in heaven's eye,* falling from time to
> time with a swoop and a sound *as if the heavens were rent, torn
> at last to very rags and tatters,* and yet a seamless cope remained;
> small imps that fill the air and lay their eggs on the ground on
> bare sand or rocks on the tops of hills, where few have found
> them; graceful and slender *like ripples caught up from the pond,
> as leaves are raised by the wind to float in the heavens;* such
> kindredship is in nature.[21]

Similes like these – especially the one in which nighthawks borne
upward are like "ripples caught up from the pond," which are, in
turn, like "leaves ... raised by the wind" – evoke a kindredship not
only between the elements of the object-world, but between the elements of the object-world and the elements of consciousness. Being
open to those forms of kindredship and bringing them to bear on the
present moment is, for Melville, a precondition of kindredship with
others, both the real-world others with whom he interacts and the
virtual Others to whom he writes.

   Understood in these terms, similes may be said to be, like
exclamations, a small-scale means of forwarding a very large project: bringing life to the lifeless, relation to the unrelated. Similes and
exclamations *stay close,* both to the statement they elaborate or intensify and to the statement's addressee, even as they give expression to

affects, memories, and fantasies that exceed the necessities of the present. They are, in Melville's work, responses to the tendency of all things to ebb and flatten, responses that are, despite their evanescence, oddly reliable; they may come and go, but they *keep* coming and going. Over time, moreover, they may be incorporated into the rhythms and textures of one's experience of Melville's writing, becoming a basic part of its maternal, transformational provisioning. Things *can* exist in excess of themselves, they whisper to us. Things *can* be ordinary in kind but exceptional in degree. There *is* something real signified by the word "just," by exclamation marks, by italics, by "like," "as," and "as if"; there *is*, both outwardly and inwardly, an amplifiability and redescribability on which we can draw. "The warmly cool, clear, ringing, perfumed, overflowing, redundant days, were *as crystal goblets of Persian sherbet, heaped up – flaked up, with rose-water snow*," Ishmael writes (*MD*, 110; emphasis added). "The starred and stately nights *seemed haughty dames in jewelled velvets, nursing at home in lonely pride, the memory of their absent conquering Earls, the golden helmeted suns!*" (110; emphasis added). Just as the days and nights of the equatorial Atlantic give of themselves, beyond necessity, to Ishmael, so does Ishmael give of himself, beyond necessity, to us.

9 Camp Melville

But if that is the case, why was *Moby-Dick*, the most bountiful of Melville's books, attacked by so many of its reviewers? Why was it attacked, in fact, *because* of its surplus provisioning, *because* of what its reviewers tended to describe as its extravagance? Here, in brief, are some examples of that line of attack, drawn from fourteen of the nineteen strongly negative reviews.

> Extravagance is the bane of the book, and the stumbling block of the author. (*London Atlas*)
>
> Having written one or two passable extravagancies, he has considered himself privileged to produce as many more as he pleases, increasingly exaggerated and increasingly dull. (*United States Magazine and Democratic Review*)
>
> Here ... comes Herman Melville ... with the old extravagance, running a perfect muck throughout the three volumes, raving and rhapsodizing in chapter after chapter. (*London Morning Chronicle*)
>
> Mr. Melville is a man of too real an imagination, and a writer with too singular a mastery over language and its resources, to have satisfied our expectations by such an extravaganza as this. (*London Examiner*)
>
> Mr. Melville has to thank himself only if his horrors and his heroics are flung aside by the general reader, as so much trash belonging to the worst school of Bedlam literature. (*London Athenaeum*)
>
> This is an odd book, professing to be a novel; wantonly eccentric; outrageously bombastic. (*London Literary Gazette*)
>
> There are few readers who will not be at first repulsed by its eccentricity. (*New York Commercial Advertiser*)

It is a crazy sort of affair, stuffed with conceits and oddities of all kinds, put in artificially, deliberately, and affectedly. (*Boston Post*)

Up to the middle of the book the writer is half the time on his head, and the other half dancing a pirouette on one toe. (*New York Independent*)

The "marvellous" injures the book by disjointing the narrative, as well as by its inherent want of interest. (*London Spectator*)

[S]tuff and nonsense [is] spouted forth by the crazy Captain. (*New York Albion*)

[Ahab's] ravings, and the ravings of some of the tributary characters, and the ravings of Mr. Melville himself, meant for eloquent declamation, are such as would justify a writ *de lunatico* against all the parties. (*Southern Quarterly Review*)

All the rules which have hitherto been understood to regulate the composition of works of fiction are despised and set at naught. (*Dublin University Magazine*)

He spreads his subject out beyond all reasonable bounds. (*Parker's Journal*)[1]

Although it is often imagined that *Moby-Dick* was primarily criticized for its impiety, that criticism was in fact much less frequent and fervent than the kind of criticism that I am identifying here.[2] The career-derailing impact of the reviews on Melville's "very susceptible and peradventure feeble temperament" is far less likely to have proceeded from the scattered references to his blasphemies than from the nearly unvarying attacks on his extravagance.[3]

Nearly unvarying. He may have read – I hope he read – a passage in which a reviewer writes that "[t]he whole work beams with the analogies of a bright and teeming fancy," another in which a reviewer writes that *Moby-Dick*'s "minute details [are] constantly enlivened and elevated by the peculiarly exalted and enthusiastic tone of the writer, by the strong flash of what we cannot but call a certain poetic light," and another in which a reviewer writes that "[t]here are descriptions in this book of almost unrivalled force, coloured and warmed as they are, by the light and heat of a most poetical imagination."[4] For each of these readers, the book's tonal and imaginative extravagance is, to some degree, a source of delight. Instead of experiencing the extravagance of *Moby-Dick* as a grandiose, dissociative negation of reality, they experience it as, in part, a bright beaming, a strong flash of light. What is revealed by that light is tellingly unspecified; it is as though what they are praising is the light itself, or perhaps a modal lighting-up, a series of lighting effects. Something in excess of reasonable bounds seems to shine out from the book at intervals for these readers, something that hints of a wealth of enlivening and elevating possibilities in the space beyond those bounds.

These three reviewers share with Melville, it seems to me, something like what Eve Sedgwick describes as "the often very fragile concern to provide the self with pleasure and nourishment in an environment that is perceived as not particularly offering them."[5] That concern with self-provisioning, or what Sedgwick describes, borrowing terminology from Melanie Klein, as the "reparative impulse," is grounded in the entirely realistic fear "that the culture surrounding it is inadequate or inimical to its nurture; it wants to assemble and confer plenitude on an object that will then have resources to offer to an inchoate self."[6] The "queer-identified practice of camp" is, for Sedgwick, an expression of this desire. Instead of associating camp with "the projects of parody, denaturalization, demystification, and mocking exposure of the elements and assumptions of a dominant culture," Sedgwick identifies its "defining elements" – "the startling, juicy displays of excess erudition, for example; the passionate, often hilarious antiquarianism, the prodigal production of alternative historiographies; the 'over'-attachment to fragmentary, marginal, waste, or leftover products; the rich, highly interruptive affective variety; the irrepressible fascination with ventriloquistic experimentation; the disorienting juxtapositions of present with past, and popular with high culture" – with the reparative impulse.[7] "What we can best learn from such practices," she writes, "are, perhaps, the many ways selves and communities succeed in extracting sustenance from the objects of a culture – even of a culture whose avowed desire has often been not to sustain them."[8]

Sedgwick's listing of the defining elements of camp evokes, with uncanny precision, many of the defining elements of *Moby-Dick*. Juicily excessive erudition ("as for my exact knowledge of the bones of the leviathan in their gigantic, full grown development, for that rare knowledge I am indebted to my late royal friend Tranquo, king of Tranque, one of the Arsacides" [344]); passionate-hilarious antiquarianism ("This whale, among the English of old vaguely known as the Trumpa whale, and the Physeter whale, and the Anvil Headed whale, is the present Cachalot of the French, and the Pottfisch of the Germans, and the Macrocephalus of the Long Words" [118]); wildly alternative historiographies ("no doubt the first man that ever murdered an ox was regarded as a murderer; perhaps he was hung; and if he had been put on his trial by oxen, he certainly would have been; and he certainly deserved it if any murderer does" [242]); inexplicable attachments to narratively insignificant things ("my friend Dr. Snodhead, a very learned man, professor of Low Dutch and High German in the college of Santa Claus and St. Pott's, to whom I handed the work for translation, giving him a box of sperm candles for his trouble – this same Dr. Snodhead, so soon as he spied the book, assured me that 'Dan Coopman' did not mean 'The Cooper' but 'The Merchant'" [342–3]); quick-switching affects ("'Oh, very severe!' chimed in the patient himself; then suddenly altering his voice, 'Drinking hot rum toddies with me every night, till he couldn't see to put on the bandages; and sending me to bed, half seas over, about three o'clock in the morning. Oh, ye stars! he sat up with me indeed, and was very severe in my diet" [338]); irrepressible ventriloquisms ("Speak out! You have seen him spout; then declare what the spout is; can you not tell water from air? My dear sir, in this world it is not so easy to settle these plain things. I have ever found your plain things the knottiest of all" [292]); and disorienting temporal and cultural juxtapositions ("Whether to admit Hercules among us or not, concerning this I long remained dubious: for though according to the Greek mythologies, that antique Crockett and Kit Carson – that brawny doer of rejoicing good deeds, was swallowed down and thrown up by a whale; still, whether that strictly makes a whaleman of him, that might be mooted" [286]) – all this, in *Moby-Dick*, is a means of self-and-audience-nourishment. It is, to return to Sedgwick's formulation, an extravagantly performative attempt to "confer plenitude on [objects] that will then have resources to offer to an inchoate self." And *Moby-Dick* is by no means the only instance in Melville's work of this kind of antic, earnest restocking of an implicitly depleted world. Take, for example, the lengthy evocation, in *Pierre*, of the thoughts that go through Pierre's mind as he stands in his closet before a portrait of his late father sitting in a chair, a portrait that was painted at a time when Pierre's father was rumored to be courting a beautiful French emigrant, a portrait that is strikingly unlike the commissioned portrait of his father that hangs in the drawing room:

> [E]ver new conceits come vaporing up in me, as I look on the strange chair-portrait: which, though so very much more unfamiliar to me, than it can possibly be to my mother, still sometimes seems to say – Pierre, believe not the drawing-room painting; that is not thy father; or, at least, is not *all* of thy father. Consider in thy mind, Pierre, whether we two paintings may not make only one. Faithful wives are ever over-fond to a certain imaginary image of their husbands; and faithful widows are ever over-reverential to a certain imagined ghost of that same imagined image, Pierre. Look again. I am thy father as he more truly was. In mature life, the world overlays and varnishes us, Pierre; the thousand proprieties and polished finenesses and grimaces intervene, Pierre; then, we, as it were, abdicate ourselves, and take unto us another self, Pierre; in youth we *are*, Pierre, but in age we *seem*. Look again. I am thy real father, so much the more truly, as thou thinkest thou recognizest me not, Pierre. To their young children, fathers are not wont to unfold themselves entirely, Pierre. There are a thousand and one odd little youthful peccadilloes, that we think we may as well not divulge to them, Pierre. Consider this strange, ambiguous smile, Pierre; more narrowly regard this mouth. Behold, what is this too ardent and, as it were, unchastened light in these eyes, Pierre? I am thy father, boy. There was once a certain, oh, but too lovely young Frenchwoman, Pierre.

Youth is hot, and temptation strong, Pierre; and in the minutest moment momentous things are irrevocably done, Pierre; and Time sweeps on, and the thing is not always carried down by its stream, but may be left stranded on its bank; away beyond, in the young, green countries, Pierre. Look again. Doth thy mother dislike me for naught? Consider. Do not all her spontaneous, loving impressions, ever strive to magnify, and spiritualize, and deify, her husband's memory, Pierre? Then why doth she cast despite upon me; and never speak to thee of me; and why dost thou thyself keep silence before her, Pierre? Consider. Is there no little mystery here? Probe a little, Pierre. Never fear, never fear. No matter for thy father now. Look, do I not smile? – yes, and with an unchangeable smile; and thus have I unchangeably smiled for many long years gone by, Pierre. Oh, it is a permanent smile! Thus I smiled to cousin Ralph; and thus in thy dear old Aunt Dorothea's parlor, Pierre; and just so, I smile here to thee, and even thus in thy father's later life, when his body may have been in grief, still – hidden away in Aunt Dorothea's secretary – I thus smiled as before; and just so I'd smile were I now hung up in the deepest dungeon of the Spanish Inquisition, Pierre; though suspended in outer darkness, still would I smile with this smile, though then not a soul should be near. Consider; for a smile is the chosen vehicle for all ambiguities, Pierre. When we would deceive, we smile; when we are hatching any nice little artifice, Pierre; only just a little gratifying our own sweet little appetites, Pierre; then watch us, and out comes the odd little smile. Once upon a time, there was a lovely young Frenchwoman, Pierre. Have you carefully, and analytically, and psychologically, and metaphysically, considered her belongings and surroundings, and all her incidentals, Pierre? Oh, a strange sort of story, that, thy dear old Aunt Dorothea once told thee, Pierre. I once knew a credulous old soul, Pierre. Probe, probe a little – see – there seems one little crack there, Pierre – a wedge, a wedge. Something ever comes of all persistent inquiry; we are not so continually curious for nothing, Pierre; not for nothing, do we so intrigue and become wily diplomatists, and glozers with our own minds, Pierre; and afraid of following the Indian trail from the open plain into the dark thickets, Pierre; but enough; a word to the wise. (*P*, 83–4; emphasis in original)

The passage feels, in Matthiessen's words, "unconsciously compelled," like a product of self-hypnotism (which would account for the thirty-three pre-punctuational "Pierres"). It moves in a dreamlike way into deeper and deeper strangenesses, both of style ("Have you carefully, and analytically, and psychologically, and metaphysically, considered her belongings and surroundings, and all her incidentals, Pierre?") and of conception ("Probe, probe a little – see – there seems one little crack there, Pierre – a wedge, a wedge"). Crucially, too, it bears witness to the interentanglement of pain and pleasure in Camp Melville, an interentanglement that is typical of camp performance more generally. However inventive and elevated a camp performance may be, it is prompted, definitionally, by a sense of something missing, something that one longs for, something whose absence hurts. When Pierre stands in front of the painting and allows himself to be "strangely alive to that certain mild mystery which invested it" (*P*, 81), what grows in him, with an increasing wildness and luxuriance, is an unconsciously longed-for alternative to the "pure, exalted idea of his father" (*P*, 82). "I am thy father as he more truly was," Pierre imagines the painting saying to him. "I am thy real father.... I am thy father, boy."

In longing for contact with his "father as he more truly was," Pierre is, obviously, longing for his sexual father, for a man with a "too ardent and, as it were, unchastened light" in his eyes. He is longing, that is, to be in relation to a sexually alive man. That longing may or may not be homosexual – it may be (who knows?) a homosocial desire to identify himself with his father's heterosexual positioning – but it is definitely queer, both "in the nineteenth-century sense of unpredictable, unusual, and unconventional" and in at least one of the

specialized modern senses of the term.⁹ The queerness of queer artists, the critic Jennifer Doyle argues, "resides not only in the domain
of the sexual but in how they make art, in the kinds of relationships
between people and art they foster."¹⁰ The value of an artist like
Melville, for Doyle, is that he provides "those of us (which is probably
most of us) who find ourselves living at odd angles with ... monolithic
structures" with a variety of "user's manuals for finding pleasure in a
world more often than not organized around that pleasure's annihila-
tion."¹¹ Pierre – who is not yet fully aware of the degree to which he is
"at odd angles" with respect to a wide range of patriarchal structures –
discovers the chair-portrait fostering in him a relationship to it, and
through it to his father, that is a source of unpredictable, unusual, and
unconventional pleasures. Readers of *Pierre*, who may or may not be
aware of their own odd angles, may discover the chair-portrait passage
fostering the same kind of thing in them.

Or not. "We are all queer customers, Mr. Duyckinck," Melville
writes in an 1850 letter, "you, I, & every body else in the world. So if I
here seem queer to you, be sure, I am not alone in my queerness, tho'
it present itself at a different port, perhaps, from other people, since
every one has his own distinct peculiarity" (*C*, 180). One can never
be certain whether, when, or how a reader will develop the kind of
relationship that Doyle has in mind, a relationship in which an object
"whose meaning seem[s] mysterious, excessive, or oblique" becomes
"a prime resource for survival," in which "sites where the meanings
[don't] line up tidily with each other" are invested "with fascination
and love."¹² One can only be certain, as a reader of Melville, that one
will repeatedly encounter the mysterious, the excessive, the oblique,
and the askew, that it will be possible, again and again, for one's own
distinct peculiarity to reverberate with Melville's. Here are a few
examples, drawn from *Mardi*, *Redburn*, and *White-Jacket*:

> West, West! West, West! Whitherward point Hope and prophet-
> fingers; whitherward, at sun-set, kneel all worshipers of
> fire; whitherward in mid-ocean, the great whales turn to die;
> whitherward face all the Moslem dead in Persia; whitherward

lie Heaven and Hell! – West, West! Whitherward mankind and empires – flocks, caravans, armies, navies; worlds, suns, and stars all wend! – West, West! – Oh boundless boundary! Eternal goal! Whitherward rush, in thousand worlds, ten thousand thousand keels! Beacon, by which the universe is steered! – Like the north-star, attracting all needles! Unattainable forever; but forever leading to great things this side thyself! – Hive of all sunsets! – Gabriel's pinions may not overtake thee!

Over balmy waves, still westward sailing! From dawn till eve, the bright, bright days sped on, chased by the gloomy nights; and, in glory dying, lent their luster to the starry skies. So, long the radiant dolphins fly before the sable sharks but seized, and torn in flames – die, burning: – their last splendor left, in sparkling scales that float along the sea. (*M*, 551)

Behold the organ!...

What sculptured arches, leading into mysterious intricacies! – what mullioned windows, that seem as if they must look into chapels flooded with devotional sunsets! – what flying buttresses, and gable-ends, and niches with saints! – But stop! 'tis a Moorish iniquity; for here, as I live, is a Saracenic arch; which, for aught I know, may lead into some interior Alhambra.

Ay, it does; for as Carlo now turns his hand, I hear the gush of the Fountain of Lions, as he plays some thronged Italian air – a mixed and liquid sea of sound, that dashes its spray in my face.

Play on, play on, Italian boy! what though the notes be broken, here's that within that mends them. Turn hither your pensive, morning eyes; and while I list to the organs twain – one yours, one mine – let me gaze fathoms down into thy fathomless eye; –'tis good as gazing down into the great South Sea, and seeing the dazzling rays of the dolphins there.

Play on, play on! for to every note come trooping, now, tri-umphant standards, armies marching – all the pomp of sound.

Methinks I am Xerxes, the nucleus of the martial neigh of all the Persian studs. Like gilded damask-flies, thick clustering on some lofty bough, my satraps swarm around me.

But now the pageant passes, and I droop; while Carlo taps his ivory knobs; and plays some flute-like saraband – soft, dulcet, dropping sounds, like silver cans in bubbling brooks. And now a clanging, martial air, as if ten thousand brazen trumpets, forged from spurs and swordhilts, called North, and South, and East, to rush to West!

Again – what blasted heath is this? – what goblin sounds of Macbeth's witches? – Beethoven's Spirit Waltz! the muster-call of sprites and specters. Now come, hands joined, Medusa, Hecate, she of Endor, and all the Blocksberg's, demons dire.

Once more the ivory knobs are tapped; and long-drawn, golden sounds are heard – some ode to Cleopatra; slowly loom, and solemnly expand, vast, rounding orbs of beauty; and before me float innumerable queens, deep dipped in silver gauzes.

All this could Carlo do – make, unmake me; build me up; to pieces take me; and join me limb to limb. He is the architect of domes of sound, and bowers of song. (R, 289–90)

Amphitheatrical Rio! in your broad expanse might be held the Resurrection and Judgment-day of the whole world's men-of-war, represented by the flag-ships of fleets – the flagships of the Phoenician armed galleys of Tyre and Sidon; of King Solomon's annual squadrons that sailed to Ophir, whence in after times, perhaps, sailed the Acapulco fleets of the Spaniards, with golden ingots for ballasting; the flag-ships of all the Greek and Persian craft that exchanged the war-hug at Salamis; of all the Roman and Egyptian galleys that, eagle-like, with blood-dripping prows, beaked each other at Actium; of all the Danish keels of the Vikings; of all the musquito craft of Abba Thule, king of the Pelews, when he went to vanquish Artingall; of all the Venetian, Genoese, and Papal fleets that came to the shock at Lepanto;

of both horns of the crescent of the Spanish Armada; of the
Portuguese squadron that, under the gallant Gama, chastised
the Moors, and discovered the Moluccas; of all the Dutch
navies led by Van Tromp, and sunk by Admiral Hawke; of the
forty-seven French and Spanish sail-of-the-line that, for three
months, essayed to batter down Gibraltar; of all Nelson's seventy-
fours that thunder-bolted off St. Vincent's, at the Nile,
Copenhagen, and Trafalgar; of all the frigate-merchantmen of
the East India Company; of Perry's war-brigs, sloops, and schoo-
ners that scattered the British armament on Lake Erie; of all the
Barbary corsairs captured by Bainbridge; of the war-canoes of the
Polynesian kings, Tammahammaha and Pomaree – ay! one and
all, with Commodore Noah for their Lord High Admiral – in this
abounding Bay of Rio these flag-ships might all come to anchor,
and swing round in concert to the first of the flood....
    When the Neversink swept in, word was passed, "Aloft, top-
men! and furl the t'-gallant-sails and royals!"
    At the sound I sprang into the rigging, and was soon at my
perch. How I hung over that main-royal-yard in a rapture! High in
air, poised over that magnificent bay, a new world to my ravished
eyes, I felt like the foremost of a flight of angels, new-lighted
upon earth, from some star in the Milky Way. (*WJ*, 211–12)

Melville offers up these kinds of extravaganzas, I think, because he
knows that the weird, wild energies in them may be, at any given
moment, in painfully short supply. Just as many "[p]eople come for
psychoanalysis when they are feeling undernourished," so do many
people come to art when "what they have been given wasn't good
enough, so they couldn't do enough with it," or when "there is something wrong with their capacity for transformation."[13] What makes
art pleasurable, in such cases, is that it provides one with the feeling
of being able – at last! – to do more with one's experience and thereby
get more out of it. In his camp-like passages, Melville is both modeling
the activity of making an insufficiently fruitful world bear the kind
of fruit that one likes and inviting us to harvest it, to use it however

we want to, to make of it what we will. The chair-portrait passage, for instance, is almost frantic in its efforts to signal that something may be made of it; five sentences begin with "Consider," four with "Look," two with "Probe," and one with "Behold." "Something ever comes of all persistent inquiry; we are not so continually curious for nothing," the painting tells Pierre, or Pierre, via the painting, tells himself. Believe that your curiosity is central to who you are and that it links you to everyone else, Melville tells us; believe that persistent inquiry will take you somewhere worth going.

What makes the negative reviews of *Moby-Dick* so chilling is the cumulative force of the pressure that they exert in the opposite direction. Extravaganzas are nothings, they declare, and nothing comes of nothing. The assuredness of their smackdowns proceeds from their awareness of how widely their opinions are shared, how common their sensibleness is, how upheld they are by the dogmatisms of a masculinist literary culture. The effects that Melville produces, writes a reviewer of *Typee*, are of a kind that are most easily produced in children, "whose fresher susceptibilities are easily made to act with force enough to get the better of their little judgments," the "ignorant," "who are but tall children," and women, "whose more nervous organization renders them prompt dupes of their own imaginations." When privileged male readers are "agitated" by "unusual and bewitching sensations," they "see no longer with the eyes of common sense," which is to say that they see no longer from the vantage point of privileged men.[14] This is why weirdness and excessiveness must be ruthlessly cut from the herd, why the negative reviewers of *Moby-Dick* never qualify their criticisms – never say, for example, that while they don't like the book's extravagance, other readers might. "[W]hat subtle power is this," asks Redburn, anticipating Carlo's performance, "that so enters, without knocking, into our inmost beings, and shows us all hidden things?" (*R*, 288). What is this seeming alienness that is at home in the deepest parts of us, that momentarily shines there? "[N]othing less," the critic Eric Auerbach writes, "than the wealth of reality and depth of life in every moment to which we surrender ourselves without prejudice."[15] This is the birthright that the negative reviewers are selling for a mess of masculinist pottage. This is why Melville writes, in an 1849 letter, that "it is [his] earnest desire to write those sort of books which are said to 'fail'" (C, 139) – because his "failings," his self-discrediting susceptibilities, his helplessly excessive creative energies, are what keep him close to "the wealth of reality and depth of life." Surrendering himself without prejudice is how he finds his way to his readers. And it can be, if we let it, how we find our way to him.

10 Courting Surprise

[Melville] is an incalculable person, full of daring & questions, & with all momentous considerations afloat in the crucible of his mind. He tosses them in, & heats his furnace sevenfold & burns & stirs, & waits for the crystallization with a royal indifference as to what may turn up, only eager for truth, without previous prejudice.

—Sophia Hawthorne

Emerging from embeddedness, finding and facing the unfamiliar, is the great task of life, accomplished over and over again in productive and satisfying lives, in ever more subtle and mature ways. One must emerge from embeddedness, or more properly, always be in the process of struggling with it, in order to "directly encounter" others and the world around one.

—Donnell Stern

Everyone involved in the trial of Adolf Eichmann, Hannah Arendt writes in *Eichmann in Jerusalem*, seemed to find it impossible "to admit that an average, 'normal' person, neither feeble-minded nor indoctrinated nor cynical, could be perfectly incapable of telling right from wrong."[1] When the judges told Eichmann, who oversaw the deportation of Eastern European Jews to concentration camps, that "all he had said was 'empty talk,'" they were under the impression that "the emptiness was feigned, and that the accused wished to cover up other thoughts, which, though hideous, were not empty."[2] In fact, Arendt argues, the emptiness of Eichmann's talk covered up nothing at all; he was "genuinely incapable of uttering a single sentence that was not a cliché." Despite "his rather bad memory," he "repeated word for word the same stock phrases and self-invented clichés (when he did succeed in constructing a sentence of his own, he thereupon repeated it until it became a cliché) each time he referred to an incident or event of importance to him."[3] "The longer one listened to him," she writes, the more obvious it became that his inability to speak was closely connected with an inability to *think*, namely, to think from the standpoint of somebody else. No communication was possible with him, not because he lied but because he was surrounded by the most reliable of all safeguards against the words and the presence of others, and hence against reality as such. (emphasis in original)[4]

The absence of thinking in Eichmann would ultimately lead Arendt to the following question, which she formulates in the opening pages of *The Life of the Mind*: "Could the activity of thinking as such, the habit of examining whatever happens to come to pass or to attract attention, regardless of results and specific content, could this activity be among the conditions that make men abstain from evil-doing or even actually 'condition' them against it?"[5]

It depends, to begin with, on what one means by thinking. For Arendt, it is a "pondering reflection [that] does not produce definitions and in that sense is entirely without results."[6] It is not "a prerogative of the few but an ever-present faculty in everybody," and although it can be "employed in the attempt to know," it is at such times "never itself ... but the handmaiden of an altogether different enterprise."[7] As opposed to being a means of arriving at completed thoughts, thinking is, she argues, a means of "unfreez[ing], as it were, what language, the medium of thinking, has frozen into thought."[8] It is not, however, a ceaseless flux; neither is it, psychically speaking, "without results." As she argues in "Some Questions Concerning Moral Philosophy," it is a "way of striking roots, of taking one's place in the world into which we all arrive as strangers."[9] Those roots are not only external but internal; anyone who has done a lot of active, creative thinking, she writes, will be "rooted in his [or her] thoughts and remembrances," will have both an orientation toward further thinking and a wealth of materials to think with.[10] "[L]imitless, extreme evil is possible only where these self-grown roots ... are entirely absent," she writes, only where people "skid ... over the surface of events," only where they are "carried away without ever penetrating into whatever depth they may be capable of."[11] She puts the case more bluntly in a 1963 letter: "the more superficial someone is, the more likely will he be to yield to evil."[12]

Melville was, in his own words, "a pondering man" (*J*, 35). The defining characteristic of a pondering person, for Melville as for Arendt, is that he or she values for its own sake the experience of "stopping ... and beginning to think," the experience of "reaching another dimension than the horizon of everyday life."[13] Pondering is promiscuous, proceeds browsingly, and only occasionally leads to a thought that one is moved to speak of. From its various bases in the mind, it rays out into experience, continually creating new circuits between perception and memory, and sometimes generating, over time, new perspectives on experience. It elicits, accordingly, both pleasure and uneasiness, both an uplifting and a dizzying feeling of being in motion. Thinking's "most dangerous aspect from the viewpoint of common sense," Arendt writes in *The Life of the Mind*, "is that what was meaningful while you were thinking dissolves the moment you want to apply it to everyday living," which is why common-sense thinking so often seems to proceed from a "desire to find results that would make further thinking unnecessary."[14] The mind incessantly "creates out of the incessant dissolvings of its own prior creations," Melville writes in *Pierre*, which is why one can never say to oneself, "I have come to the Ultimate of Human Speculative Knowledge; hereafter, at this present point I will abide" (*P*, 167). "[S]o true is this," he goes on to say, "that some men refuse to solve any present problem, for fear of making still more work for themselves in that way" (*P*, 205).

What Melville most profoundly shares with Arendt is a feel for the way in which thought emerges out of and segues into thinking. In response to an editor's commentary on John Milton's "wanderings in belief," Melville wrote, in the margins of his Milton volume, "[h]e who thinks for himself never can remain of the same mind."[15] The value of the thinking process, a process that operates throughout our species and beyond, is that it makes it possible to be something other than the same old self, to find oneself in new conjunctions with others. The more attuned we become to the thinking process, the more aware we become that each thought has, as William James argues, a "halo or penumbra that surrounds and escorts it," a "fringe" that consists of "the sense of its relations, near and remote, the dying echo of whence it came to us, the dawning sense of whither it is to lead."[16] And the more aware we become of those vapory extensions beyond the body of the thought – the more we sense in ourselves the movement toward a thought and then past it – the more aware we become of each thought's non-finality. "Really, universally, relations stop nowhere," writes Henry James.[17] Whatever one says or does creates the possibility of further saying or doing; whatever one perceives creates the possibility of further perceptions.

Racism is, to say the least, a freezer of thoughts and a limiter of relations. In Morrison's *The Bluest Eye*, the white storekeeper, Mr. Yacobowski, "urges his eyes out of his thoughts to encounter" the young girl who has come up to the counter. "Somewhere between retina and object," however, "his eyes draw back, hesitate, and hover."[18] Pecola "looks up at him and sees the vacuum where curiosity ought to lodge. And something more. The total absence of human recognition – the glazed separateness."[19] Racism suspends curiosity and hangs out, as the sign of that suspension, a glazed expression, the expression of someone who is either not looking at anything at all or is looking at something that can only be one thing. "All things in [Pecola] are flux and anticipation," Morrison writes. "But her blackness," in the eyes of white people, "is static and dread."[20]

Thinking is, by contrast, an unfreezer of thoughts and an expander of relations. "It is a frightful poetical creed that the cultivation of the brain eats out the heart," Melville writes in an 1851 letter to Hawthorne. "But it's my *prose* opinion that in most cases, in those men who have fine brains and work them well, the heart extends down to the hams" (C, 192; emphasis in original). There is no need for the Hawthornean opposition of head and heart; one can "stand for the heart" (C, 192), as Melville does, and stand for the head as well, as long as the head is understood as a means of extending and deepening a capacity for relations. If one not only knows but feels that each thought has a history and a future, that each thought – each perception, each statement – is a momentary crystallization of an endless distillate, one can allow oneself to move outward, onward, past each point of arrival, toward the perception beyond the first perception, the thought beyond the first thought, the statement beyond the first statement. Whatever someone else appears to be upon first thought, or upon second thought, or upon third, is never all that he or she is.

Most white nineteenth-century writers resist that kind of perceptual/interpretive movement in their representations of non-white characters. Here, for example, is how we are introduced to pivotal non-white characters in James Fenimore Cooper's *The Pioneers* (1823) and Harriet Beecher Stowe's *Dred* (1856):

> [They] beheld, standing at one of the distant doors of the hall, the person of [Chingachgook]....
>
> The instant that [he] observed himself to be noticed by the group ... he dropped the blanket which covered the upper part of his frame, from his shoulders, suffering it to fall over his leggins of untanned deer-skin, where it was retained by a belt of bark that confined it to his waist.
>
> As he walked slowly down the long hall, the dignified and deliberate tread of the Indian surprised the spectators. His shoulders, and body to his waist, were entirely bare, with the exception of a silver medallion of Washington, that was suspended from his neck by a thong of buckskin, and rested on his high chest, amid many scars. His shoulders were rather broad and full; but the arms, though straight and graceful, wanted the muscular appearance that labor gives to a race of men. The medallion was the only ornament he wore, although enormous slits in the rim of either ear, which suffered the cartilages to fall two inches below the members, had evidently been used for the purposes of decoration in other days. In his hand he held a small basket of the ash-wood slips, colored in divers fantastical conceits, with red and black paints mingled with the white of the wood.[21]
>
> There was a crackling in the swamp, and a movement among the copse of briers; and at last the speaker emerged, and stood before Harry. He was a tall black man, of magnificent stature and

proportions. His skin was intensely black, and polished like marble. A loose shirt of red flannel, which opened very wide at the breast, gave a display of a neck and chest of herculean strength. The sleeves of the shirt, rolled up nearly to the shoulders, showed the muscles of a gladiator. The head, which rose with an imperial air from the broad shoulders, was large and massive, and developed with equal force both in the reflective and perceptive department. The perceptive organs jutted like dark ridges over the eyes, while that part of the head which phrenologists attribute to the moral and intellectual sentiments, rose like an ample dome above them. The large eyes had that peculiar and solemn effect of unfathomable blackness and darkness which is often a striking characteristic of the African eye. But there burned in them, like tongues of flame in a black pool of naphtha, a subtle and restless fire, that betokened habitual excitement to the verge of insanity. If any organs were predominant in the head, they were those of ideality, wonder, veneration, and firmness; and the whole combination was such as might have formed one of the wild old warrior prophets of the heroic ages. He wore a fantastic sort of turban, apparently of an old scarlet shawl, which added to the outlandish effect of his appearance. His nether garments, of coarse negro-cloth, were girded round the waist by a strip of scarlet flannel, in which was thrust a bowie-knife and hatchet. Over one shoulder he carried a rifle, and a shot-pouch was suspended to his belt. A rude game-bag hung upon his arm.[22]

Instead of flux and anticipation, we get stillness: in Dred's case, an actual motionlessness, and in Chingachgook's case, a slow, stately, expressionless walk down a long hall. The meticulousness of the attention to physiology, clothing, and accoutrements makes it seem as though those details are both indexical and comprehensive, as though everything that there is to know about these characters can be conveyed, in a paragraph or two, by those means. Instead of unfreezing the frozen and unglazing the glazed, Cooper and Stowe invite their implicitly white reader to behold stable, familiar spectacles, to be interested in what Chingachgook and Dred will do, perhaps, but not in who they – and the reader – might become. Chingachgook and Dred are important to the plots of the novels, but they neither inspire nor demand the kind of open-ended interest on which living relationships are based.

These passages are, obviously, racist. However, given the degree to which racism and anti-racism are, at present, conceptualized in moral terms, we should try to say something more than that about them. When moral outrage is our predominant response to racism, we both limit the range of analytical tools that can be brought to bear on the issue – sociological, historical, aesthetic, psychological, etc. – and implicitly identify anti-racism with a superior moral capacity. As Arendt so compellingly argues, however, goodness alone will not save us, insofar as it can be, and often is, generated out of non-thinking, out of "hold[ing] fast to whatever the prescribed rules of conduct may be at a given time in a given society." When push comes to shove, "the readiest to obey will be those who were the most respectable pillars of society, the least likely to indulge in thoughts," because what they have gotten used to, in their essentially compliant goodness, "is less the content of the rules, a close examination of which would always lead them into perplexity, than the *possession* of rules under which to subsume particulars."[23] The lesson of "the total moral collapse of respectable society during the Hitler regime" is "that under such circumstances those who cherish values and hold fast to moral norms and standards are not reliable; we now know that moral norms and standards can be changed overnight, and that all that then will be left is the mere habit of holding fast to something."[24] Refusing "to make up [one's] mind anew" when "confronted with some difficulty," Arendt writes, "can wreak more havoc than all the evil instincts taken together."[25]

If racism is less an evil to be countered by goodness than an immobilization to be countered by movement, a superficiality to be countered by depth, then it may be more useful, as well as more accurate, to describe passages like Cooper's and Stowe's as racist *manifestations* of a resistance to thinking, in Arendt's broad, life-oriented sense of the term. Most of the white people in a racist culture who write about non-white people have internalized the idea that there is little or nothing to see or say about non-white people, that there is no need to activate the process of thinking that carries those writers into unexpected places at other moments in their work. That phenomenon is continuous with and underpins a basic fact of life in a racist culture: that many white people, including many self-nominated anti-racists, bring to their encounters with non-white people the assumption that there will be, in those encounters, few or no fringes of possibility. The advances that "racist" and "anti-racist" white people make toward non-white people are, on the whole, not as curious-minded, not as persistently interested, not as oriented toward halos and penumbras, as the advances that they make toward white people. We need, accordingly, another way of conceptualizing anti-racism, one that is less about being good than about wanting life to be life at every turn: wanting life to open, in every encounter, from perception onto perception onto perception, from thought onto thought onto thought.[26]

Melville provides us with a useful starting point for that reconceptualization in "The Spouter-Inn," the chapter in which the reader first encounters the most pivotal non-white character in *Moby-Dick*. In the bedroom of the Spouter-Inn in which Ishmael has been lodged by the landlord, a bedroom that has already been rented out to an unknown harpooner, Ishmael is about to fall asleep when a footfall and a light in the hallway arouse him. Into the room walks the harpooner, a candle in one hand and an embalmed Maori head in the other. Without noticing Ishmael in the bed, he begins struggling to open his bag. "I was all eagerness to see his face," says Ishmael,

> but he kept it averted for some time while employed in unlacing the bag's mouth. This accomplished, however, he turned round – when, good heavens! what a sight! Such a face! It was of a dark, purplish, yellow colour, here and there stuck over with large blackish looking squares. Yes, it's just as I thought, he's a terrible bedfellow; he's been in a fight, got dreadfully cut, and here he is, just from the surgeon. But at that moment he chanced to turn his face so towards the light, that I plainly saw they could not be

sticking-plasters at all, those black squares on his cheeks. They
were stains of some sort or other. (33–4)

"At first," Ishmael says, "I knew not what to make of this" (34). Then,
however, "an inkling of the truth" occurs to him: "I remembered a
story of a white man – a whaleman too – who, falling among the can-
nibals, had been tattooed by them. I concluded that this harpooneer,
in the course of his distant voyages, must have met with a similar
adventure." Having made something of what he has seen, he takes a
philosophical step back from it: "And what is it, thought I, after all!
It's only his outside; a man can be honest in any sort of skin" (34).

A moment later, however, an overlooked detail comes to mind,
the state of not knowing "what to make of this" revives, and he steps
back into the uncertainty of the experience: "But then, what to make
of his unearthly complexion, that part of it, I mean, lying round about,
and completely independent of the squares of tattooing. To be sure, it
might be nothing but a good coat of tropical tanning; but I never heard
of a hot sun's tanning a white man into a purplish yellow one" (34).
Then the harpooner takes off his hat, and Ishmael almost "sing[s] out
with fresh surprise. There was no hair on his head – none to speak of
at least – nothing but a small scalp-knot twisted up on his forehead.
His bald purplish head now looked for all the world like a mildewed
skull." Again the uncertainty revives: "I am no coward," he says, "but
what to make of this head-peddling purple rascal altogether passed
my comprehension" (34). Earlier in the chapter, standing in front of
the painting in the Spouter-Inn's entryway, Ishmael had been darted
through by idea after idea, each of which arose out of and subsided
back into uncertainty. Something similar is happening here.

And it just keeps happening. Even after getting "a good look"
at him (31) – his chest, his arms, his back, his legs – and reaching
the conclusion that he is "some abominable savage or other" (34),
the curiosity that makes Ishmael want to see more overpowers
the fear that makes him want to flee. "[He] went about something
that completely fascinated my attention"; "I now screwed my eyes
hard ... to see what was next to follow" (35). Only when the harpooner "[springs] into bed with [him]" does he cry out, and when

the landlord comes into the room, giving him the chance to leave, it takes only "a moment" for him to decide to stay (35–6). Ishmael does not, of course, say whether he and the harpooner, Queequeg, have sex that night. But he does say, at the beginning of the next chapter, that he woke to find Queequeg's arm "thrown over me in the most loving and affectionate manner" (36), an arm whose tattooing and variegated tanning makes it blend in with the blanket, which is "full of odd little parti-colored squares and triangles" (37). Queequeg keeps inspiring Ishmael with "fresh surprise" and Ishmael keeps sensing in Queequeg an unmethodical heterogeneity that commingles with the heterogeneity of the object-world – keeps having, in other words, a disorienting, pleasurable "what to make" feeling about him, a feeling that is at the very least continuous with erotic feeling. The childhood memory that comes to Ishmael's mind at this moment, the memory of waking in the middle of the night to find his hand being held by the hand of "nameless, unimaginable, silent form or phantom" (37), evokes not only his investment in the experience of being held by Queequeg, but also his association of Queequeg with everything that is fringe-like, penumbral, not-yet known – everything that makes further thinking possible.

The value of all this is thrown into sharp relief by the "Metaphysics of Indian-Hating" section of *The Confidence-Man*, in which Charlie Noble tells the cosmopolitan the story of the back-woodsman John Moredock. The defining feature of Indian-haters, Charlie says, is that they obsess over a "signal outrage" until "the thought develops such attraction, that much as straggling vapors troop from all sides to a storm-cloud, so straggling thoughts of other outrages troop to the nucleus thought, assimilate with it, and swell it" (*CM*, 180). In Moredock's case, that nucleating process began when he was told in the middle of a meal that his family had been killed by Indians. He "kept eating, but slowly and deliberately, chewing the wild news with the wild meat, as if both together, turned to chyle, together should sinew him to his intent. From that meal he rose an Indian-hater" (183). By assimilating to itself whatever vapory fringes of thought were in its vicinity, the "nucleus thought" became, in Moredock, a swollen, changeless center of psychic gravity. Never again did Moredock feel the need to think, in the active, relational, disseminatory sense of the term, about Indians; he just killed them. Even after becoming, years later, "restored to the ordinary life of the region and period," he "never let pass an opportunity of quenching an Indian" (184).

He was not, however, "naturally ferocious" (184), any more than Eichmann was. "On the contrary," Charlie says, he "was an example of something apparently self-contradicting, certainly curious, but, at the same time, undeniable: namely, that nearly all Indian-haters have at bottom loving hearts" (185). In his relations with white people, Moredock was so "convivial," "[h]ospitable," "benevolent," and "courteous," and eventually so "admired and loved," that he was elected to the Illinois territorial council and "pressed to become candidate for governor" (185–6). Metaphysically speaking, Moredock's core characteristic, the characteristic from which all other characteristics proceeded, was not his racism but his commitment to the immobilization of thought. By arresting the process of thinking, establishing a walled-in psychic location where the fixed idea of Indian outrages could be, in William James's words, "held before the mind for an indefinite time, and contemplated without changing," Moredock became the kind of person who could unquestioningly and wholeheartedly participate in the preservation of the existing social order. Killing Indians, turning them into entities with which there could be no further relations, was of a piece with doing what society expected him to do: contribute to the smooth functioning of a world without surprises.[27]

"We all ... have [a] permanent consciousness of whither our thought is going," William James writes. "It is a feeling like any other, a feeling of what thoughts are next to arise, before they have arisen."[28] Our consciousnesses are, in fact, "in very large measure constituted of *feelings of tendency*, often so vague that we are unable to name them."[29] Allowing ourselves to be drawn by those feelings of tendency into thought after thought after thought, surrendering ourselves to the process of making up our minds anew, enables us to become better attuned to the transitive, as opposed to the substantive, dimensions of experience. It also enables us, as Arendt suggests, to strike deeper roots in the world. Living our experiences in an intense, attentive, open-ended way – being curious, persistently inquiring – gives us more to work with and makes us more capable of working with it. "When the analyst questions what he thinks he already knows about the patient, and about his reactions to the patient, uncertainty is preserved," Donnell Stern writes. "It becomes harder to feel convinced of any single answer. These conditions constitute the climate in which unbidden perceptions flourish. In trying to create them, the analyst is doing what is possible to court surprise."[30] By courting surprise, by bringing a readiness for experience, an interest in perceptual/interpretive movement, everywhere one goes, one can create, as Melville puts it in *Mardi*, "the creative," a capacity to discover and articulate more than what immediately appears. A "person who seeks security ... uproots himself from the present moment, the only thing that *is*, and so he becomes a perpetual drifter," writes the critic James Breslin.[31] A person who courts surprise roots herself in the present moment, in a curiosity about where it comes from and where it will go. She may, when push comes to shove, hold her ground.

11 All Things Trying

> A copse skirting the road was just bursting out in bud. Each unrolling leaf was in the very act of escaping from its prison. Israel looked at the budding leaves, and round on the budding sod, and up at the budding dawn of the day.
>
> —Melville, *Israel Potter*

> How to extricate what Melville blindly knew and did from what he merely said, kept turning his mind to, or tossed up as material for his novels and poems. How to show ... that sort of blindness of his which continues to make *him* valuable, not his surfaces. Make a try.
>
> —Charles Olson

I have been presenting Melville's works as, in the critic Philip Davis's words, "a means of opening and reopening, innerly shifting and deepening, mental pathways" – a means of taking oneself beyond "acceptable social attitudes and the habitual stories of one's self."[1] I have, in addition, been presenting Melville's works as a continually renewed effort to generate, out of pure successiveness, a feeling for form. I have been arguing, finally, that what matters more than the individual instances of formal completion – the well-turned phrases, the aria-like chapters, the compact, disciplined poems – is the persistence in that effort. For me, as for the poet Charles Olson, one of the greatest of Melville's values is that he "drove further than any of his predecessors toward forcing totality of effort to yield some principle out of itself."[2] "I try all things," Ishmael tells us. "I achieve what I can" (*MD*, 273).

The principle yielded up by Melville's totality of effort is, in part, that all things may be tried – that consciousness never stops seeking opportunities for creative activity and that the world never stops supplying those opportunities. "Nothing was now inert fact," Olson writes, with respect to Melville's conception of existence. "[A]ll things were there for feeling, to promote it, and be felt."[3] But the principle is, in addition, that *all things are trying*. For Melville, Olson argues, "man, in the midst of it, knowing well how he was folded in, as well as how suddenly and strikingly he could extend himself ... was suddenly possessed or repossessed of a character of being a thing among things, which I shall call his physicality.... Reality was without interruption."[4] Everything is folded in; everything is capable of suddenly, strikingly extending itself; everything wants, as Hurston writes in *Their Eyes Were Watching God*, to "show [its] shine."[5]

Part of what Melville's totality of effort enabled him to do, in other words, was to sense, as he composed, the degree to which life, all around him, was ongoingly composing itself. In "The Apple-Tree Table" (1856), Melville's narrator sees, after a night-long vigil alongside an inexplicably ticking table – a table that contains, unbeknownst to him, long-ago-laid beetle eggs – "a short nibbled sort of crack, from which (like a butterfly escaping its chrysalis), the sparkling object, whatever it might be, was struggling. Its motion was the motion of life. I stood becharmed."[6] The motion of life is present not only in the struggling of the folded-in beetle, but also in the responsiveness of the narrator, who is, all at once, too thrilled to move, too riveted to turn away. It is present, as well, in the coming-to-existence of the sentences that I have quoted, both at the moment of writing and, potentially, at the moment of reading. Each of these things is a "sparkling object"; each is an instance of what the philosopher Gilles Deleuze describes as "active force," which "affirms its difference and makes its difference an object of enjoyment and affirmation."[7] "Each hung bell's/Bow swung finds tongue to fling out broad its name," writes Gerard Manley Hopkins. "Each mortal thing does one thing and the same;/Deals out that being indoors each one dwells," crying, "*Whát I do is me: for that I came.*"[8]

Everywhere in Melville's work, that cry resounds. When White-Jacket, about to be scourged, is swayed by a desire to knock the captain overboard, he describes it as an "instinct" that is identical with an "instinct diffused through all animated nature, the same that prompts even a worm to turn under the heel" (*WJ*, 280). In the poem "Venice," Melville writes that coral insects are impelled to build reefs by the same "Pantheistic energy of will" that impelled Venetians to build "reefs of castles"; in the lecture "Statues in Rome," he writes that the idealizations of "riderless and rearing" horses in ancient Greek statuary are proof of the "enlarged humanity of that elder day, when man gave himself none of those upstart airs of superiority over the brute creation which he now assumes."[9] "Trust me," Babbalanja says in *Mardi*, "there are more things alive than those that crawl, or fly, or swim. Think you ... there is no sensation in being a tree? feeling the sap in one's boughs, the breeze in one's foliage? think you it is nothing to be a world? one of a herd, bison-like, wending its way across boundless meadows of ether?" (*M*, 458). Upon feeling his ship bound forward, as if each "mast and timber" has "a pulse in it that [is] beating with life and joy," Redburn feels himself bounding forward too, under the influence of "a wonderful thing in [him], that responded to all the wild commotion of the outer world; and went reeling on and on with the planets in their orbits, and was lost in one delirious throb at the center of the All" (*R*, 76).

And so on. Few artists have so consistently attempted to indicate what Deleuze describes as "an opening for life, a path between the cracks."[10] Even fewer have dramatized the movement through those cracks – the Emersonian "shooting of the gulf" or "darting to an aim" – with such urgency and joy.[11] Take, for instance, the following chapter-opening from *The Confidence-Man*:

> The sky slides into blue, the bluffs into bloom; the rapid
> Mississippi expands; runs sparkling and gurgling, all over in
> eddies; one magnified wake of a seventy-four. The sun comes out,
> a golden huzzar, from his tent, flashing his helm on the world. All
> things, warmed in the landscape, leap. Speeds the dædal boat as a
> dream. (*CM*, 94)

We can most easily track the paragraph's movement by focusing on its successive surprises. To begin with, the sky, which is rarely the agent of an action, "slides," and what it slides into, unpredictably, is "blue." The next clause accelerates the movement through contraction – the omission of the verb – but also slows it through alliteration ("blue ... bluffs ... bloom") and syntactic parallelism ("into blue ... into bloom"). The river, too, is in unexpected motion; instead of merely flowing, it "expands." As if in response, Melville's narrator grows expansive, giving a more detailed description of the river's transformation ("sparkling and gurgling, all over in eddies") and, in a figurative escalation, comparing it to a large naval vessel's transformation of the ocean's surface ("one magnified wake of a seventy-four"). The sun steps forth, giving rise to another figurative escalation ("a golden huzzar, from his tent, flashing his helm on the world"), and then everything beneath it steps forth as well ("All things, warmed in the landscape, leap"). The final sentence of the paragraph reestablishes the steamboat as the focal setting of the novel, evokes its participation in this all-involving motion, and provides, by means of a dropped grammatical subject and a look-it-up word, a climactic stylistic flourish ("Speeds the dædal boat as a dream"). In just sixty-seven words, Melville has enabled us to make imaginative contact with a vital, pluralistic world, a world in which all things are leaping.

Each of the political positions that Melville takes up over the course of his career may be understood as an expression of his solidarity with that world, his resistance to the diminishment of life's leapings. At the heart of his opposition to colonialists and missionaries in the Pacific, for instance, is that they situate Pacific islanders at such a vast conceptual remove that the islanders can no longer be perceived as fellow beings, as unique instances of a universal stepping-forth. This is what makes it possible for the members of the US Exploring Expedition to flatten a Fijian village and then call "upon all Christendom to applaud their courage and their justice" (T, 27), or for an American missionary's wife to hitch two Hawaiian men to a go-cart and rap them on their heads with the handle of her fan when they can't make it up a hill. "Will the tender-hearted lady, who has left friends and home for the good of the souls of the poor heathen, will she think a little about their bodies and get out, and ease [them] until the ascent is mounted?" Melville asks. "Not she; she could not dream of it" (T, 189). There are a great many bodies in the Pacific islands to be thought about, and each of those bodies is, as Deleuze writes, "composed of a plurality of irreducible forces."[12] The reality of those active forces never seems to touch the consciousnesses of colonialists and missionaries, however, and it is even farther from the consciousnesses of most of the freebooting white sailors in the Pacific, who "hardly consider [the islanders] human."[13] Hence Melville's sympathy with "the spirit which prompts the Typee warrior to guard all the passes to his valley with the point of his levelled spear, and, standing upon the beach, with his back turned upon his green home, to hold at bay the intruding European" (T, 196).

Hence too his sympathy, in White-Jacket, with sailors who resist the arbitrariness and absoluteness of naval discipline. In addition to devoting four early chapters to a diatribe against flogging, White-Jacket spends four late chapters on the "melancholy recital" of what he describes as "The Massacre of the Beards" (WJ, 355). After the captain of the USS Neversink sees "the setting sun, streaming in at the port-holes, [light] up every hair" on the sailors' heads, "till … the two long, even lines of beards seemed one dense grove," he orders them to shorten their hair and trim their beards (356, 357). All the sailors protest, but most of them allow the ship's barbers to shave them clean. There are, however, a few older sailors who insist on retaining their beards and who are, accordingly, summoned to face the captain at the main-mast. "Such an array of beards!" White-Jacket cries, when the resisters are all standing in a row before the captain: "spade-shaped, hammer-shaped, dagger-shaped, triangular, square, peaked, round, hemispherical and forked" (363). Fifteen minutes later, all but one of the non-conformists has allowed his beard to be shaved off. The solitary hold-out, Ushant, is flogged and sent to the brig, where he sits out the remainder of the voyage, his long gray beard untouched. While in the brig, White-Jacket says, Ushant spends "many hours in braiding his beard, and interweaving with it strips of red bunting, as if he desired to dress out and adorn the thing which had triumphed over all opposition" (366).

Why do the beards matter to Melville? Because they are expressions of active force – which, again, "affirms its difference and makes its difference an object of enjoyment and affirmation" – and because their loss is a loss of diversity, which is indispensable to our "multiform pilgrim species" (CM, 14).[14] The massacre of all but one of the

Neversink's beards may be seen as, in Arendt's words, "an attack upon human diversity as such, that is, upon a characteristic of the 'human status' without which the very words 'mankind' or 'humanity' would be devoid of meaning."[15] The same may be said of the way in which the paper-making machine in Melville's "The Paradise of Bachelors and the Tartarus of Maids" (1855) affects its young, "sheet-white" female operatives.[16] As a result of their prolonged subordination to "the metallic necessity, the unbudging fatality that governed [the machine]," the operatives have become, tragically, its "tame minister[s]."[17] "Before my eyes," Melville's narrator says, while watching the machine produce paper, "I seemed to see, glued to the pallid incipience of the pulp, the yet more pallid faces of all the pallid girls I had eyed that heavy day. Slowly, mournfully, beseechingly, yet unresistingly, they gleamed along, their agony dimly outlined on the imperfect paper, like the print of the tormented face on the handkerchief of Saint Veronica."[18] In place of the partial likenesses that enable the sideways-hopping movement of similes – including the story's structural simile, which links the Paradise of Bachelors in London to the Tartarus of Maids in western Massachusetts – there is just more of the same: pallid pulp that gives rise to "yet more pallid faces," all of which are versions of a single "tormented face." In place of exclamatory self-extension, there is only necessity, fatality, and an "agony dimly outlined."

In each of the above instances, the crisis is the same: whether it is in colonies, missionary settlements, navies, or factories – or slave-ships, prisons, slums, etc. – what is besieged is active force and the unity-in-diversity that it brings into the world.[19] It is, for Melville, a crisis with simultaneously individual and social dimensions. In an individual context, it entails suffering – the bearing of a pain of indefinite duration – and an at least partial loss of the ability to share a world with others. In "The Piazza" (1856), Melville's lonely narrator discovers in a hillside cabin an even more lonely young woman, Marianna, for whom the activity of thinking has devolved into "[t]hinking, thinking" – an endless, barren cycling, "a wheel [she] cannot stop." Catching sight of "a far-off, soft, azure world" – the farmland that he has just come from – the narrator says to Marianna, "You must find this view very pleasant." "Oh sir," she says, "the first time I looked out of this window, I said 'never, never shall I weary of this.'" "And what wearies you of it now?" he asks. "I don't know," she says, "but it is not the view, it is Marianna."[20] Withdrawn from the world, and then withdrawn still further by her suffering, Marianna has lost the capacity to make something of her perceptual experience; she now brings nothing but weariness to it and extracts nothing but weariness from it. Near the end of the story, she directs the narrator's attention to two hop-vines that seem to have tried and failed to touch and intertwine. It is as if, the narrator writes, having reached the tips of their separate poles, the vines "would have then joined over in an upward clasp, but the baffled shoots, groping awhile in empty air, trailed back whence they sprung."[21] If what we see in moving water is, as Ishmael tells us in the opening chapter of *Moby-Dick*, "the ungraspable phantom of life" (*MD*, 20), then what we are presented with in the image from "The Piazza" is the obverse scenario, in which one sees nothing more than the frozen, separate elements of what could have, but did not, combine to generate a new and renewable life.

The social dimension of the crisis is, as I have already suggested, the threat that it poses to human diversity. If the uniqueness of each human being were to lose its significance – if uniformity were to be preferred to it – the concept of humanity, which is, definitionally, a unification of a plurality, would lose its significance as well. "Seat thyself sultanically among the moons of Saturn, and take high abstracted man alone; and he seems a wonder, a grandeur, and a woe," Ishmael writes. "But from the same point, take mankind in mass, and for the most part, they seem a mob of unnecessary duplicates" (*MD*, 356). Although the first of those two ways of "taking" humankind may seem too romantic, the second one is, for Melville, too terrible to accept. "[A]s out of the crude forms of the natural earth [the priests] could evoke by art the transcendent mass & symmetry & unity of the pyramid," he writes in his journal after an 1856 visit to the Great Pyramid, "so out of the rude elements of the insignificant thoughts that are in all men, they could rear the transcendent conception of a God. But for no holy purpose was the pyramid founded" (*J*, 78). By sucking the rudiments of thinking up into the single, unchanging thought of God and embodying that thought in the "transcendent mass & symmetry & unity of the pyramid," the priests violate the plurality and ambiguity of not-yet-formulated thoughts. In doing so, they attack what Arendt calls "worldly reality," which can only appear "where things can be seen by many in a variety of aspects without changing their identity, so that those who are gathered around them know they see sameness in utter diversity." "The end of the common world has come," she writes, "when it is seen only under one aspect and is permitted to present itself in only one perspective."[22]

The sapping of active force by weariness, the compression of worldly plurality into sameness – these are the looming psychosocial possibilities against which Melville most often bends his energies. At times, as I have indicated, he does so by evoking and intensifying the animating leaping of all things. At other times, however, he does so by trying to get us to recoil from the nightmarish prospects of social isolation and conformity. He knows very well that there are people who have no "respect for the fact of pain," who sense it, in themselves and others, "but will not suffer it and so cannot be said to discover it."[23] He also knows very well that there are people who have no respect for the fact of diversity, who register the endlessly ramifying otherness of existence but will not accept its decentering of the self. In his moments of greatest despair, when he retreats to the cave of pessimism, Melville is, temporarily, somewhat like those people; he flees the specificity of suffering through philosophical generalizations and flees the indeterminacy of otherness by ruling out the possibility of change. Again and again, however, he finds his way back. It is not just Suffering that he writes about in *Moby-Dick* but the particular sufferings of characters like Perth and Pip. And it is not just Otherness that he writes about in "Bartleby" and "Benito Cereno" but an otherness that cannot easily be swept up into otherness in general, an otherness that haunts, that exceeds one's capacity to locate and name it. He does not blithely assert the inherent vitality of all things; he cherishes each instance of it, lives its experience to the limits of his powers, and retains an acute awareness of how vulnerable it is.

"I believe there is something sleeping beneath the chaos [of American life] that is of extraordinary value, if only we have the courage to go down and bring it up," James Baldwin says in a 1962 interview.²⁴ What sleeps down there, Baldwin suggests, is the explanation of "why the lives we lead on this continent are mainly so empty, so tame, and so ugly" – which is that white Americans have conditioned themselves not to be sensual, not to "respect and rejoice in the force of life," in order to fend off any awareness of their violation of that force in their treatment of black and native peoples.²⁵ If white Americans could only acknowledge the fact of that violation, they might, Baldwin speculates, be able to acknowledge the related fact that the world is neither white nor white-centered. They might then be more willing to have open-ended, sensually alive interactions with others, interactions that are less limited by a gravitation toward safety and power, interactions in which they are moved by "something active, something ... like a fire, like the wind, something which can change [them]."²⁶ The hope that Melville feels, with respect to national and global futures, has a similar, and similarly unstable, basis. There is much, maybe too much, to overcome – too much suffering, too much stasis, too much uniformity. And yet something in Melville cannot help believing that something like a fire, like the wind, can transfigure the world's pyramidical consolidations of power. In an 1852 letter to Nathaniel Hawthorne, he calls *The Blithedale Romance*, Hawthorne's recently published satire of utopian aspirations, "an antidote to the mooniness of some dreamers – who are merely dreamers – Yet who the devel [sic] aint a dreamer?" (*C*, 231). What is politics without utopia? What is life without dreaming? And what good is any perspective on existence that does not take in the testimony of every self-extending thing around us, that does not seek to join each of those testimonies, imaginatively, in an upward clasp? Over there is the pyramid, massive, symmetrical, and unitary. Over here, however, in a more intimate region of Melville's mind, is a subtle, insistent counter-display. Scud, overleaping the rock against which a wave has broken. Grass, upsprouting between the seams of flagstones. A horse, riderless and rearing. A beetle, struggling through a crack. Coral insects, building reefs. Baffled shoots, groping into the air. A worm, turning under the heel. A whale, shooting lengthwise from the sea. A leaf, escaping from its prison. The budding sod, the budding dawn. A coffin, upbursting from a shipwreck, on which one can, for a little while, float.

12 The Noncommunicating Central Self

[P]asted on one side wall [of Melville's desk], well out of sight, was a printed slip of paper that read simply, "Keep true to the dreams of thy youth."

If we but knew what these dreams were! That they grew out of the deepest needs of the whole man seems certain. That they reflected a desire to nourish the roots of life, I believe.

—Eleanor Melville Metcalf

I somehow cling to the strange fancy, that, in all men, hiddenly reside certain wondrous occult properties ... [that] may chance to be called forth here on earth; not entirely waiting for their better discovery in the more congenial, blessed atmosphere of heaven.

—Melville, "Hawthorne and His Mosses"

"Do you want to know how I pass my time?" Melville asks Evert Duyckinck in a December 1850 letter.

I rise at eight – thereabouts – & go to my barn – say good-morning to the horse, & give him his breakfast. (It goes to my heart to give him a cold one, but it can't be helped.) Then, pay a visit to my cow – cut up a pumpkin or two for her, & stand by to see her eat it – for it's a pleasant sight to see a cow move her jaws – she does it so mildly and with such a sanctity. – My own breakfast over, I go to my work-room & light my fire – then spread my M.S.S. [*Moby-Dick*] on the table – take one business squint at it, & fall to with a will. At 2 1/2 P.M. I hear a preconcerted knock at my door, which (by request) continues till I rise & go to the door, which serves to wean me effectively from my writing, however interested I may be. My friends the horse & cow now demand their dinner – & I go & give it to them. (*C*, 174)

The quietness of these *Moby-Dick* days is remarkable. He says "good morning" to his horse, watches his cow move her jaws, has a breakfast that seems not to register in his consciousness, and then goes upstairs and writes "with a will" until there is a knock, which eventually awakens him from his trance. Back, then, to his "friends the horse & cow." After his own dinner, he writes, "I rig my sleigh & with my mother or sisters start off for the village" to get the mail (*C*, 174). That pretty much does it for social interaction. "My evenings," he writes, "I spend in a sort of mesmeric state in my room – not being able to read – only now & then skimming over some large-printed book" (*C*, 174).

There is in each of us, D. W. Winnicott proposes, a "non-communicating central self," a part of us that "never communicates with the world of perceived objects, and that ... must never be communicated with or be influenced by external reality."[1] It is of course true that "healthy persons communicate and enjoy communicating," Winnicott writes, but it is also true "that *each individual is an isolate, permanently non-communicating, permanently unknown, in fact unfound*" (emphasis in original).[2] It often seems to me, when reading *Moby-Dick*, that Melville is unusually in touch with this part of himself, not just because he writes with such forcefulness about "*Isolatoes*" and isolatedness (*MD*, 107), but because it so often seems that, to return to the image from Yeats's poem, his mind is moving on silence. Although Melville would represent the interior of the innermost chamber of the mind as an emptiness in *Pierre*, and although one can feel the pull of that nihilistic conclusion in *Moby-Dick* as well ("the lid there's a sounding-board; and what in all things makes the sounding-board is this – there's naught beneath" [395]), the abundance of *Moby-Dick* overwhelmingly bears witness to the generativity of the quietness out of which it was written. Underlying all of *Moby-Dick*'s energetic improvisations is a silence that must be safeguarded, because, paradoxically, "in health, it is out of this that communication naturally arises."[3]

An even more powerful example of Melville's writing-from-silence, however, is *Billy Budd*, the uncompleted manuscript that was found in his desk after his death. The three characters at its

center – Billy Budd, Captain Vere, and John Claggart – are isolatoes in a more extreme sense than any of the characters in *Moby-
Dick*. Each is, in a word that Melville uses heavily in *Billy Budd*,
"phenomenal," which is to say that each is inexplicable in ordinary
terms. In each of them is something that cannot be accounted for
biographically, psychologically, sociologically, philosophically, polit-
ically, or theologically. In each of them, too, is a strong inward vec-
toring, expressed in Vere and Claggart through a shared preference
for privacy and secrecy and in Billy through an "organic hesitancy"
of speech at moments of excitement.[4] Most importantly, the narrator, though he at times adopts a familiar, tale-telling tone, seems, in
general, to be writing from a great and constant distance, from somewhere near the rim of the horizon of human experience. It was one of
the dreams of Melville's youth, or at least of his early manhood, that
there are "certain wondrous occult properties" in everyone and that
they may, under certain circumstances, be called forth. In *Billy Budd*,
he evokes, for himself and for whoever may ultimately be reading his
words, the wondrousness of what may be developed in human beings
out of their noncommunicating central selves. But he evokes, as well,
the ultimate athwartness, with respect to society, of those absolutely
silent selves. The form that he never finished feeling his way toward
in *Billy Budd* seems to have become, near the end, one in which
those two evocations could be brought into a quasi-musical relation
with one another.

I am trying to call attention to an orientation in *Billy Budd*
that lies somewhere to the side of the conflicts that are usually said
to be at the heart of Melville's final work – the conflict between
freedom and social order, say, or between natural and positive law.
The orientation that I have in mind is most closely related to the one
that the critic Michael Warner identifies in his reading of "Shiloh:
A Requiem (April 1862)," one of the best-known poems in *Battle-
Pieces*. Here is the poem:

> Skimming lightly, wheeling still,
>   The swallows fly low
> Over the field in clouded days,

> The forest-field of Shiloh –
> Over the field where April rain
> Solaced the parched ones stretched in pain
> Through the pause of night
> That followed the Sunday fight
> Around the church of Shiloh –
> The church so lone, the log-built one,
> That echoed to many a parting groan
> And natural prayer
> Of dying foemen mingled there –
> Foemen at morn, but friends at eve –
> Fame or country least their care:
> (What like a bullet can undeceive!)
> But now they lie low,
> While over them the swallows skim,
> And all is hushed at Shiloh.[5]

In the poem's crucial parenthetical line, Warner notes, "[w]e are not told who is deceived about what.... The bullet strips away conviction and habit, and we are not told much about what kind of subjectivity is left."[6] And yet, Warner argues, "[w]hat appears to be a subject imagined only in the radically negative state of undeception is in fact vested with a richly unintegrated subjectivity," for "this excavation of inwardness happens in the scene of a suddenly bonded mass of male friends, stretched toward one another in a mutually witnessing physicality that has been intensified to the utmost extremity."[7] Like Walt Whitman's "The Wound-Dresser," which also pivots on a "great lingering parenthesis" – "(Many a soldier's loving arms about this neck have crossed and rested./Many a soldier's kiss dwells on these bearded lips.)" – "Shiloh" creates, Warner writes, "a subject for whom eros, mortality, and the witnessing of injury must be protected against the closure of redemption. In both poems, Christian frameworks of bellicose redemption enter into visible conflict with a distinctive picture of subjective experience and a baseline sanctification of life."[8]

Many readings of *Billy Budd* are dominated by frameworks, Christian and otherwise, of "bellicose redemption," and in support of those readings, passages signifying some degree of commitment to "the closure of redemption" are plucked and collated ("At the same moment it chanced that the vapory fleece hanging low in the East was shot through with a soft glory as of the fleece of the Lamb of God seen in mystical vision, and simultaneously therewith, watched by the wedged mass of upturned faces, Billy ascended, and, ascending, took the full rose of the dawn" [124]; "'With mankind,' [Vere] would say, 'forms, measured forms are everything; and that is the import couched in the story of Orpheus with his lyre spellbinding the wild denizens of the wood'" [128]). Many other readings are built around passages that seem to encourage a "radically negative state of undeception" ("unobstructed agency on equal terms – equal superficially, at least – soon teaches one that unless upon occasion he exercise a distrust keen in proportion to the fairness of the appearance, some foul turn may be served him" [87]; "[the military chaplain] indirectly subserves the purpose attested by the cannon ... he lends the sanction of the religion of the meek to that which practically is the abrogation of everything but brute Force" [122]). But the feel of the story as a whole is far removed from the spirit of such passages, is much closer to what Warner describes, with respect to "Shiloh," as an "unmastered expressivity."[9] Billy Budd began as a poem with a headnote, and grew, through successive additions to the headnote, into its present hypercephalic form. Even more than in Moby-Dick, Melville is making it up as he goes along, and making it up, for the most part, backwards. There are scattered moments in Billy Budd in which the attainment of redemption or undeception is presented to us as a real and attractive possibility, but the story as a whole repeatedly draws back from its own prospects of finalization. Billy Budd in its entirety predominantly evokes, like "Shiloh," a "richly unintegrated subjectivity," an attunement to "eros, mortality, and the witnessing of injury," and "a distinctive picture of subjective experience and a baseline sanctification of life."

I am thinking about passages like these:

> Not at first did Billy take it in. When he did, the rose-tan of
> his cheek looked struck as by white leprosy. He stood like one

impaled and gagged. Meanwhile the accuser's eyes removing
not as yet from the blue dilated ones, underwent a phenomenal
change, their wonted rich violet color blurring into a muddy
purple. Those lights of human intelligence losing human expression, gelidly protruding like the alien eyes of certain uncatalogued
creatures of the deep. (98)[10]

In contrast with the funereal hue of these surroundings the prone
sailor's exterior apparel, white jumper and white duck trousers,
each more or less soiled, dimly glimmered in the obscure light of
the bay like a patch of discolored snow in early April lingering at
some upland cave's black mouth. (118–19)

The silence at the moment of execution and for a moment or two
continuing thereafter, a silence but emphasized by the regular
wash of the sea against the hull or the flutter of a sail caused
by the helmsman's eyes being tempted astray, this emphasized
silence was gradually disturbed by a sound not easily to be verbally rendered. Whoever has heard the freshet-wave of a torrent
suddenly swelled by pouring showers in tropical mountains,
showers not shared by the plain; whoever has heard the first muf-
fled murmur of its sloping advance through precipitous woods,
may form some conception of the sound now heard. (125–6)

[W]hen the tilted plank let slide its freight into the sea, a second
strange human murmur was heard, blended now with another
inarticulate sound proceeding from certain larger seafowl who,
their attention having been attracted by the peculiar commotion
in the water resulting from the heavy sloped dive of the shotted
hammock into the sea, flew screaming to the spot. So near the
hull did they come, that the stridor or bony creak of their gaunt
double-jointed pinions was audible. (126–7)

Each of these passages is an instance of "tak[ing] it in," of living the
experience for which one is finding words. In *Israel Potter*, Melville's

narrator, momentarily stationed at a distance from a naval battle, tells us that "in the deeper water, was a lurid cloud, incessantly torn in shreds of lightning, then fusing together again, once more to be rent," and that in order to "get some idea of the events enacting in that cloud, it will be necessary to enter it; to go and possess it, as a ghost may rush into a body" (*IP*, 141). In the first of the above passages, when the narrator of *Billy Budd* enters the cloud of Billy's consciousness in order to "get some idea of the events enacting in [it]," he registers, first of all, a color-transition: a "rich violet color blurring into a muddy purple." Then, in a hypnotic fragment, that metamorphosis blurs into other metamorphoses: from the human to the nonhuman, from expressiveness to vacancy, from warmth to gelidity, from planarity to protrusion, from the terrestrial to the oceanic, from classifiability to unclassifiability. The narrator is not trying to add to the narrative's symbolic depth or thematic complexity; he is trying to take the unmastered expressivity in Claggart's eyes so deeply into himself that he can bring it out in a similarly unmastered form – so that he can intensify the disorienting feeling of passing between states.

The same may be said of the three other passages, each of which invites us, first and foremost, to participate in associatively rich forms of moment-to-moment perception. Whiteness, soiled, dimly glimmers – discolored snow lingers at a cave's black mouth. Silence, silence, emphasized silence, gradually disturbed by a sound – between trees, down a mountainside, pours a shower-swelled torrent. Plank tilts, corpse slides, sailors murmur – the screaming of seafowl, the bony creak of their pinions. In a 1914 description of how he composed the two-line poem "In a Station of the Metro" – "The apparition of these faces in the crowd;/Petals on a wet, black bough" – Ezra Pound writes,

> Three years ago in Paris I got out of a "metro" train at La Concorde, and saw suddenly a beautiful face, and then another and another, and then a beautiful child's face, and then another beautiful woman, and I tried all that day to find words for what this had meant to me, and I could not find any words that seemed to me worthy, or as lovely as that sudden emotion. And that

evening, as I went home along the Rue Raynouard, I was still
trying and I found, suddenly, the expression. I do not mean that
I found words, but there came an equation ... not in speech, but
in little splotches of colour.... In a poem of this sort, one is trying
to record the precise instant when a thing outward and objective
transforms itself, or darts into a thing inward and subjective.[11]

At what precise instant does a thing outward transform itself or dart
into a thing inward? What is worthy of, or as lovely as, certain sudden perceptions and the feelings that accompany them? Trying to
answer such questions, trying to follow one's steps and flights, is, or
can become, a life's work, in which one addresses oneself again and
again to small-m forms of meaningfulness: instants with durational
dimensions, apparations with psychic fringes. "The great revelation
had never come," Woolf writes in *To the Lighthouse*. "The great revelation perhaps never did come. Instead there were little daily miracles, illuminations, matches struck unexpectedly in the dark."[12] Like
Woolf – like a great many of us, artists and otherwise – Melville tries
to convey, even if only to himself, the value of these moments of
being, when life unexpectedly stands still here.

That "here" is, as Woolf suggests, never the space of the great
revelation, never coextensive with the Truth of redemption or undeception. The value of that kind of Truth, pragmatically speaking,
is that it stimulates movements of consciousness in the midst of
which a match is struck, an illumination occurs, and one momentarily knows where one is. In a well-known notebook entry, Nathaniel
Hawthorne reports meeting Melville in England in 1856 and getting
into a discussion with him on "everything that lies beyond human
ken." "It is strange," Hawthorne writes,

how he persists – and has persisted ever since I knew him, and
probably long before – in wandering to-and-fro over these deserts,
as dismal and monotonous as the sand hills amid which we were
sitting. He can neither believe, nor be comfortable in his unbelief;
and he is too honest and courageous not to try to do one or the
other.[13]

Although this description is often praised for its accuracy, it misses a vital dimension of Melville's relationship to belief and unbelief: the incidental rewards of his persistent wanderings between those poles, the unanticipated blossomings that he courts and encounters in his passages to and fro. "The greatest, grandest things are unpredicted," Melville wrote in the margins of his copy of Milton's *Paradise Regained*.[14] If one can "become unintegrated," Winnicott writes, if one can "flounder" – if the noncommunicating central self can feel sufficiently safe – the greatest, grandest things may happen.[15] One may have "a sensation or an impulse" that "feel[s] real and [is] truly a personal experience."[16] One may figure out ways of having it again and again and again. One may create out of it an idiomatic, generative way of having a life.

In the poem that ends *Billy Budd*, a rougher, saltier version of Billy, close to sleep on the night before his execution, speaks from a state so remote from the sphere of agential subjects that the sensations and impulses arising in it do indeed feel like radically personal experiences of this kind:

Good of the Chaplain to enter Lone Bay
And down on his marrow-bones here and pray
For the likes just o' me, Billy Budd. – But look:
Through the port comes the moonshine astray!
It tips the guard's cutlass and silvers this nook;
But 'twill die in the dawning of Billy's last day.
A jewel-block they'll make of me tomorrow,
Pendant pearl from the yardarm-end
Like the eardrop I gave to Bristol Molly –
O, 'tis me, not the sentence they'll suspend.
Ay, ay, all is up; and I must up too,
Early in the morning, aloft from alow.
On an empty stomach now never it would do.
They'll give me a nibble – bit o' biscuit ere I go.
Sure, a messmate will reach me the last parting cup;
But, turning heads away from the hoist and the
    belay,

Heaven knows who will have the running of me up!
No pipe to those halyards. – But aren't it all sham?
A blur's in my eyes; it is dreaming that I am.
A hatchet to my hawser? All adrift to go?
The drum roll to grog, and Billy never know?
But Donald he has promised to stand by the plank;
So I'll shake a friendly hand ere I sink.
But – no! It is dead then I'll be, come to think.
I remember Taff the Welshman when he sank.
And his cheek it was like the budding pink.
But me they'll lash me in hammock, drop me deep.
Fathoms down, fathoms down, how I'll dream fast
   asleep.
I feel it stealing now. Sentry, are you there?
Just ease these darbies at the wrist,
And roll me over fair!
I am sleepy, and the oozy weeds about me twist. (132)

In his just-beginning dream, in which he feels ocean-floor weeds twisting about him, Billy rolls away from both the closure of redemption
and the clarity of undeception. Things are no longer grand. We are
neither in the speculative space of divine "magnanimity" in which
Billy and Vere, "two of great Nature's nobler order," embrace (115),
nor in the midst of the mythopoetic drama of Billy's execution. We
are down in the weeds, whose ooziness blurs the distinction between
skin and plant and whose twisting motion is a ceaseless response to
its surroundings. The sensibility we inhabit is richly, but also ter-
rifyingly, unintegrated. The expressivity is unmastered. The music
of Melville's language – which harmonizes, here as elsewhere, with
the openness and lonesomeness of the noncommunicating central
self – is coming to an end. "[W]hen I waked," Caliban says, "I cried
to dream again."[17]

Notes

INTRODUCTION

1. Louis Becke, "Introduction," *Moby-Dick* (London: Putnam's, 1901), iv.

2. See, in this context, Paul Lauter's reflections on the relationship between Melville's reputation as a "densely allusive composer whose most precious treasures [will] be yielded up ... only to learned initiates" and his students' "distaste for Melville." "For them," he writes, "the modernist preference for difficult, indeed obscure, texts ... reflect[s] a process, deeply inflected by class standards, whose effect is to marginalize them culturally.... Melville was constructed as ... an icon of an academic reading community toward which my undergraduates feel deep suspicion" (*From Walden Pond to Jurassic Park: Activism, Culture, and American Studies* [Durham, NC: Duke University Press, 2001], 217, 218, 219).

3. I am drawing language here from my essay "The Tale That Won't Let Go," *O Magazine* (July 2006), 164.

4. Bob Hoover, "'Hard Books,' Easy Lessons from Oprah," *Pittsburgh Post-Gazette*, July 9, 2006.

5. Ibid.

6. Edgar A. Dryden, to take only one example, closes his study of Melville with the claim that "dark sayings" are, for Melville, "the defining mark of the literary, the mark that inevitably sets it apart from the conditions of its appearance, its cultural context, or local circumstantial history" (*Monumental Melville: The Formation of a Literary Career* [Stanford, CA: Stanford University Press, 2004], 194).

7. Allan's father was Major Thomas Melvill, who participated in the Boston Tea Party; Maria's father was General Peter Gansevoort, who

repulsed the British attack on Fort Stanwix. The final "e" was added to the Melvill family name after Allan's death.

8. In 1835, he attended Albany Classical School in the spring and in 1836–7, he attended Albany Academy for six months. After the age of twelve, in other words, he only received about nine months of formal education.

9. "HERMAN MELVILLE CRAZY," in *New York Day Book*, September 7, 1852, reprinted in Brian Higgins and Hershel Parker, eds., *Herman Melville: The Contemporary Reviews* (New York, NY: Cambridge University Press, 1995), 436.

10. Marilynne Robinson, *Housekeeping* (New York, NY: Farrar, Straus, and Giroux, 1980), 19.

11. Cormac McCarthy, *The Road* (New York, NY: Vintage, 2006), 187.

12. Rita Felski offers an especially forceful statement of the theory of reading that underlies this theory of criticism: "Reading ... is a matter of attaching, collating, negotiating, assembling – of forging links between things that were previously unconnected. It is not a question of plumbing depths or tracing surfaces ... but of creating something new in which the reader's role is as decisive as that of the text. *Interpretation becomes a coproduction between actors that brings new things to light rather than an endless rumination on a text's hidden meanings or representational failures*" (*The Limits of Critique* [Chicago, IL: University of Chicago Press, 2015], 173–4 [emphasis in original]).

13. Adam Phillips, *The Beast in the Nursery: On Curiosity and Other Thoughts* (New York, NY: Vintage, 1998), xiii.

14. David Foster Wallace, *Infinite Jest* (New York, NY: Little, Brown, 1996), 379.

I LIVING THE EXPERIENCE

1. Raymond Williams, *The Long Revolution* (New York, NY: Harper & Row, 1961), 25, 34.

2. I am thinking here of the philosopher John Dewey's distinction between recognition and perception. "Bare recognition is satisfied when a proper tag or label is attached," Dewey writes. "It involves no stir of the organism, no inner commotion. But an act of perception proceeds by waves that extend serially throughout the entire organism.... Perception is an act of the going-out of energy in order to

receive, not a withholding of energy.... We must summon energy and pitch it at a responsive key in order to *take* in" (*Art as Experience* [New York, NY: Perigree, 2005], 55; emphasis in original).

3. Herman Melville, *The Confidence-Man* (New York, NY: Penguin, 1990), 104. Subsequent references will be to this edition and will be cited parenthetically with the abbreviation *CM*.

4. Alfred Kazin, "Introduction," reprinted in Richard Chase, ed., *Melville: A Collection of Critical Essays* (Englewood Cliffs, NJ: Prentice Hall, 1962), 48.

5. Herman Melville, *White-Jacket* (Evanston, IL: Northwestern University Press, 2000), 249. Subsequent references will be to this edition and will be cited parenthetically with the abbreviation *WJ*.

6. William Blake, *The Marriage of Heaven and Hell* (New York, NY: Dover, 1994), 32.

7. Gerard Manley Hopkins, journal entry, in Catherine Phillips, ed., *Gerard Manley Hopkins: The Major Works* (New York, NY: Oxford University Press, 2002), 209.

8. Herman Melville, *Moby-Dick* (New York, NY: Norton, 2002), 422. Subsequent references will be to this edition and will be cited parenthetically with the abbreviation *MD*.

9. Dewey, *Art as Experience*, 38 (emphasis in original).

10. Herman Melville, *Typee* (Boston, MA: Houghton Mifflin, 2004), 27. Subsequent references will be to this edition and will be cited parenthetically with the abbreviation *T*.

11. Dewey, *Art as Experience*, 41 (emphasis in original).

12. The critic Colin Dayan has recently made a similar observation: "We find in Melville's prose an extraordinary compression, even when he most seems to digress. Although it does not define action, it sharpens our appetite for seeing and knowing, while it suggests something unseen behind what is seen and heard. Mood replaces certainty. We are left with an all but intelligible feeling. Or is it another kind of intelligibility?" ("Melville's Creatures, or Seeing Otherwise," in *American Impersonal: Essays with Sharon Cameron*, ed. Branka Arsic [New York, NY: Bloomsbury, 2014], 56).

13. Herman Melville, *Correspondence*, ed. Lynn Horth (Evanston and Chicago: Northwestern University Press/Newberry Library, 1993), 193. Subsequent references will be to this edition and will be cited parenthetically with the abbreviation *C*.

14. Herman Melville, *Mardi* (Evanston, IL: Northwestern University Press, 1998), 595. Subsequent references will be to this edition and will be cited parenthetically with the abbreviation *M*.

2 HE KNEW NOT WHAT IT WOULD BECOME

1. Herman Melville, "Hawthorne and His Mosses," in John Bryant, ed., *Tales, Poems, and Other Writings* (New York, NY: Modern Library, 2001), 62.
2. "[F]orm," Samuel Otter reminds us, "is an object of sense as well as thought" ("Reading *Moby-Dick*," in Robert S. Levine, ed., *The New Cambridge Companion to Herman Melville*, [New York, NY: Cambridge University Press, 2014], 83). See also Elisa Tamarkin's evocation of the way in which Melville's poems, like Claude Lorrain's paintings, "create a vibratory movement ... that harmonizes its parts into tonal arrangements" ("Melville with Pictures," 173).
3. Christopher Bollas, *Cracking Up: The Work of Unconscious Experience* (New York, NY: Hill and Wang, 1995), 80.
4. Sylvia Plath, *The Journals of Sylvia Plath* (New York, NY: Anchor, 1998), 109–10.
5. Nathaniel Hawthorne, *A Wonder-Book for Boys and Girls*, in *Tales and Sketches* (New York, NY: Library of America, 1982), 1268, 1270.
6. Herman Melville, *Pierre* (New York, NY: Penguin, 1996), 284–5. Subsequent references will be to this edition and will be cited parenthetically with the abbreviation *P*.

3 GRIEF'S FIRE

1. Walter Benjamin, "The Storyteller," in *Illuminations*, trans. Harry Zohn (New York, NY: Schocken, 1968), 86.
2. Eve Kosofsky Sedgwick, *Tendencies* (Durham, NC: Duke University Press, 1993), 126.
3. Benjamin, "The Storyteller," 87.
4. Melville, "The Coming Storm," in Bryant, *Tales*, 357.
5. Phillips, *The Beast in the Nursery*, 110.
6. Melville, "Lone Founts," in Bryant, *Tales*, 535.
7. Herman Melville, *Redburn* (New York, NY: Modern Library, 2002), 11. Subsequent references will be to this edition and will be cited parenthetically with the abbreviation *R*.
8. In the standard edition of Melville's correspondence, the final clause of the passage that I have just quoted reads: "a very susceptible and peradventure *febrile* temperament" (emphasis added). There is no textual basis for the suppression of the word "feeble," which is the word that appears in Julian Hawthorne's transcription of the

never-recovered letter in *Nathaniel Hawthorne and His Wife*, 2 vols. (Boston, MA: Houghton Mifflin, 1893), 1:400. The editors seem to have changed "feeble" to "febrile" for no other reason than that they didn't like thinking about Melville as a feeble person, a person who was easily overwhelmed, a person who found it difficult to resist the pressure of outside influences.

9. Cynthia Ozick, "Judging the World," *New York Times Book Review* (March 16, 2014), 12.

4   SUSCEPTIBILITIES

1. Late in the book, Melville transforms Pierre into an author and satirizes him for operating on the basis of just such a premise. "I will write such things – I will gospelize the world anew, and show them deeper secrets than the Apocalypse!" Pierre cries, echoing King Lear, who cries, as the storm approaches, "I will do such things – /What they are, yet I know not: but they shall be/The terrors of the earth" (2.2.469–71).

2. The theory is not Melville's alone. John Dewey, to take only one example, argues that "no thought, no idea, can possibly be conveyed as an idea from one person to another.... The communication may stimulate the other person to realize the question for himself and to think out a like idea, or it may smother his intellectual interest and suppress his dawning effort at thought. But what he *directly* gets cannot be an idea. Only by wrestling with the conditions of the problem at first hand, seeking and finding his own way out, does he think" (*Democracy and Education* [New York, NY: Macmillan, 1916], 159–60 [emphasis in original]).

3. Sigmund Freud, "Recommendations to Physicians Practicing Psycho-analysis," in Peter Gay, ed., *The Freud Reader* (New York, NY: Norton, 1989), 360.

4. Christopher Bollas, *The Freudian Moment* (London: Karnac, 2007), 28.

5. Melville, "Bartleby, the Scrivener," in Bryant, *Tales*, 66. Subsequent references will be to this edition and will be cited parenthetically.

6. Dan McCall, *The Silence of Bartleby* (Ithaca, NY: Cornell University Press, 1989), 153.

7. In *Mardi*, after telling us that ships at a distance are "invisible in the full flood of noon," Melville's narrator observes that the same may be said of "other distant things: the more light you throw on them,

the more you obscure. Some revelations show best in a twilight" (*M*, 56). By shining a noon-like light on the incidental details of his encounters with Bartleby, the lawyer shields himself from his growing awareness of the richly twilit situation that he and Bartleby, on the basis of their "common humanity," share.

8. In a 1964 essay, James Baldwin argues that Shakespeare found his poetry through "knowing, which is not the same thing as understanding, that whatever was happening to anyone was happening to him" ("This Nettle, Danger … " in *Collected Essays* [New York, NY: Library of America, 1998], 691). That peculiar kind of knowledge, a knowledge-without-understanding of the resonance between oneself and "anyone," is what Melville makes available to us in "Bartleby."

9. Melville, "Benito Cereno," in Bryant, *Tales*, 256. Subsequent references will be to this edition and will be cited parenthetically.

10. There are nine manners, eight moods, five demeanors, four airs, four aspects, three postures, three tones, two appearances, and one mien.

11. Melville, "Hawthorne and His Mosses," 51. Yvor Winters, for instance, claims that "[t]he morality of slavery is not an issue in the story; the issue is this, that through a series of acts of performance and of negligence, the fundamental evil of a group of men, evil which normally would have been kept in abeyance, was freed to act" (*Maule's Curse: Seven Studies in the History of American Obscurantism* [Norfolk, CT: New Directions, 1938], 77). Although that argument grew less common as the century advanced, it did not disappear. "As a projection of the unknown in man," Ruth Mandel writes, "the blacks in 'Benito Cereno' symbolize his buried, disguised drives for power, self-gratification and violence" ("The Two Mystery Stories in 'Benito Cereno,'" *Texas Studies in Literature and Language* 24 [1973], 637). For Terry Martin, the story's message is that "to ignore evil is a dangerous thing to do, for whether it is in the wilderness without or the even murkier one within, the beast in the jungle eventually leaps" ("The Idea of Nature in *Benito Cereno*," *Studies in Short Fiction* 30 [1993], 168).

12. See, for instance, Paul Downes, "Melville's *Benito Cereno* and the Politics of Humanitarian Intervention," *South Atlantic Quarterly* 103 (2004), 465–88 and my *The Sign of the Cannibal: Melville and the Making of a Postcolonial Reader* (Durham, NC: Duke University Press, 1998).

13. In a recent example of this approach to the story, Shari Goldberg suggests that "if, at the story's end, it is impossible to say where the truth has left its mark on the story, if the reader is only aware

that something, 'neither veiled nor unveiled,' has flit through the text and disturbed him or her, like an inquietude that rises from the repose of the ordered words on the page, stymying their explanations and illuminations, then it may have testified, almost in spite of itself, after all" (*Quiet Testimony: A Theory of Witnessing from Nineteenth-Century American Literature* [New York, NY: Fordham University Press, 2013], 114).

14. See, in this context, James S. Leonard, Thomas Tenney, and Thadious M. Davis, eds., *Satire or Evasion? Black Perspectives on Huckleberry Finn* (Durham, NC: Duke University Press, 1991).

15. Toni Morrison, "This Amazing, Troubling Book," in Stephen K. George, ed., *Ethics, Literature and Theory: An Introductory Reader* (Lanham, MD: Rowman and Littlefield, 2005), 281, 283.

16. William James, *The Principles of Psychology*, 2 vols. (New York, NY: Dover, 1950), 1:252, 1:251.

17. Donnell Stern, *Unformulated Experience: From Dissociation to Imagination in Psychoanalysis* (New York, NY: Psychology Press, 2003), 36–7.

18. Ibid., 37.

19. As Christopher Freeburg rightly observes, there is no way around the fact that Melville "emphatically resists any coherent and verifiable position on slavery" in "Benito Cereno." What Melville provides, in its place, is an immersive, relational experience of "blackness," one that is "both metaphysical and social, abstract and concrete, certain in its existence and, like the enslaved Africans, mysterious and radically unpredictable" (*Melville and the Idea of Blackness: Race and Imperialism in Nineteenth-Century America* [New York, NY: Cambridge University Press, 2012], 129, 131).

20. Maurice Lee similarly argues that "when pressing political questions become tangled in metaphysical knots, Melville does not fall into skeptical silence. He defers, instead, to the future" ("Melville's Subversive Political Philosophy: 'Benito Cereno' and the Fate of Speech," *American Literature* 72 [2000], 512).

21. Melville, "Misgivings," in Bryant, *Tales*, 337.

5 DISPORTINGS

1. Christopher Bollas, *Forces of Destiny: Psychoanalysis and Human Idiom* (London: Free Association Books, 1989), 2.

2. Ibid., 86 (emphasis in original).
3. Bollas, *Being a Character: Psychoanalysis and Self Experience* (New York, NY: Hill and Wang, 1992), 59; Bollas, *Forces of Destiny*, 8.
4. Adam Phillips, *On Flirtation* (Cambridge: Harvard University Press, 1994), 158.
5. Bollas, *Forces of Destiny*, 93.
6. Ibid., 111.
7. Ibid.
8. Christopher Bollas, *The Evocative Object World* (New York, NY: Routledge, 2009), 85.
9. "Freud's theory of free association is actually – if we think about it – a theory of mental life. When we think about things to ourselves we move from one thing to another in an endless sequelae of thoughts" (Bollas, *The Freudian Moment*, 16).
10. Christopher Bollas, *The Shadow of the Object: Psychoanalysis of the Unthought Known* (New York, NY: Columbia University Press, 1987), 33.
11. Ibid., 39, 29.
12. Ibid., 258.
13. Bollas, *Forces of Destiny*, 70.
14. Marion Milner, *On Not Being Able to Paint* (London: Routledge, 2010), 88–9.
15. Heinrich von Kleist, "On the Gradual Fabrication of Thoughts While Speaking," in Philip B. Miller, ed., *An Abyss Deep Enough: Letters of Heinrich von Kleist with a Selection of Essays and Anecdotes* (New York: Dutton, 1982), 218–19.
16. Marion Milner, *The Hands of the Living God* (London: Hogarth, 1969), 384–5.
17. Bollas, *The Evocative Object World*, 85; Bollas, *Forces of Destiny*, 111.
18. Elizabeth Savage, "What We Talk Around When We Talk About The Dick," *Feminist Teacher* 21 (2011), 95–6.
19. Bollas, *Cracking Up*, 177, 167.
20. Ibid., 71.

6 A NEW WAY OF BEING HAPPY

1. Bollas, *Being a Character*, 57.
2. Ibid., 58–9 (emphasis in original).
3. William Butler Yeats, *Selected Poems and Three Plays*, ed. M. L. Rosenthal (New York, NY: Macmillan, 1962), 193–4.

4. Charles Altieri, *The Particulars of Rapture: An Aesthetics of the Affects* (Ithaca, NY: Cornell University Press, 2003), 192.

5. Ibid.

6. D. W. Winnicott, *Playing and Reality* (London: Routledge, 1991), 120, 125–6.

7. Ibid., 122.

8. Virginia Woolf, *To the Lighthouse* (New York, NY: Harcourt, 1927), 110.

9. Ibid., 113.

10. Warner Berthoff, *The Example of Melville* (New York, NY: Norton, 1972), 89.

11. The allusion is to G. Wilson Knight's "The Othello Music," in which Knight evokes the distinctiveness of *Othello*'s aural forms; the play's language is "highly-coloured, rich in sound and phrase, stately," he writes, but with "an inward aloofness of image from image, word from word" (*The Wheel of Fire: Interpretations of Shakespearean Tragedy* [New York, NY: Oxford University Press, 1930], 117, 110).

12. F. O. Matthiessen, *American Renaissance: Art and Expression in the Age of Emerson and Whitman* (New York, NY: Oxford University Press, 1941), 426.

13. Ibid.

14. "Reading the transcribed narratives of survivors' experiences during the terrorist attacks on the World Trade Center," Ghislaine Boulanger writes, "[Charles] Strozier was struck by the fact that the accounts appeared to have been spoken in iambic pentameter.... Meter, [like] anything basic to experience, begins in the self and has corporeal, physical, sensual, even sexual dimensions.... In reciting the story of what has happened to him in a basic poetic meter, the survivor reestablishes ties to the fundamental rhythm of his unbroken self" (*Wounded by Reality: Understanding and Treating Adult Onset Trauma* [New York, NY: Psychology Press, 2007], 90).

15. Elizabeth Bishop, quoted in Lloyd Schwartz and Sybil P. Estess, *Elizabeth Bishop and Her Art* (Ann Arbor, MI: University of Michigan Press, 1983), 288.

16. Woolf, *To the Lighthouse*, 161.

7 THE MEANING OF *MOBY-DICK*

1. Herman Melville, *Clarel*, eds. Harrison Hayford, Alma A. MacDougall, Hershel Parker, and G. Thomas Tanselle (Evanston and Chicago, IL: Northwestern University Press/Newberry Library, 1991), 2.26.51.

2. Bollas, *The Shadow of the Object*, 37, 24–5.
3. Ibid., 15–17.
4. Ibid., 16.
5. Toni Morrison, *Beloved* (New York, NY: Vintage, 2004), 11.
6. Ibid., 11.
7. Ibid., 276.
8. Ibid., 311.
9. Michael Eigen, *The Electrified Tightrope* (London: Karnac, 2004), 112.

8 AS IF!

1. Marilynne Robinson, *Gilead* (New York, NY: Picador, 2004), 31–2 (emphasis in original).
2. Rosi Braidotti, *Nomadic Theory: The Portable Rosi Braidotti* (New York, NY: Columbia University Press, 2011), 95.
3. Evert Duyckinck, review of *Redburn*, *The Literary World* (November 17, 1849), reprinted in Higgins and Parker, *Herman Melville*, 278.
4. Nathaniel Parker Willis, *Hurry-Graphs; or, Sketches of Scenery, Celebrities and Society, Taken from Life* (Auburn and Rochester, NY: Alden and Beardsley, 1856), 224 (emphasis in original).
5. Herman Melville, *Journals*, eds. Howard C. Horsford and Lynn Horth (Evanston and Chicago, IL: Northwestern University Press/Newberry Library, 1989), 10. Subsequent references will be to this edition and will be cited parenthetically with the abbreviation *J*.
6. Zora Neale Hurston, *Their Eyes Were Watching God* (New York, NY: Harper, 2006), 112.
7. Edgar Allan Poe, "The Philosophy of Composition," in *Essays and Reviews* (New York, NY: Library of America, 1984), 15.
8. These marginal comments appeared in Melville's volumes of Ralph Waldo Emerson's writings and may be found in transcribed and reproduced form at *Melville's Marginalia Online*. The comments were prompted by passages in "Spiritual Laws," *Essays: First Series*, 131; "Heroism," *Essays: First Series*, 228; "Illusions," *The Conduct of Life*, 201; and "Considerations by the Way," *The Conduct of Life*, 162.
9. Nowhere is this more true than in his characterization of Ahab. Forty-two percent of Ahab's sentences – 473 out of 1,116 – end in

exclamation points, an indication of the degree to which his function is to communicate to others an energy that is beyond his control. Here are a few examples: "Avast!"(111), "Good!" (137), "Corkscrew!" (138), "Hoot!" (139), "O head!" (249), "A flaw!" (371), "Science!" (378), "Rat-tat!" (396), "Thy hand!—Met!" (399), "Brace forward! Up helm!" (404), "There she blows! there she blows!—there she blows!—there she blows! There again!—there again!" (408).

10. Richard Henry Dana, Jr., *Two Years before the Mast* (New York, NY: Penguin, 1981), 416.

11. Seamus Heaney, *The Redress of Poetry* (New York, NY: Farrar, Straus, & Giroux, 1995), 158.

12. William James, *A Pluralistic Universe* (Cambridge: Harvard University Press, 1977), 129.

13. Theo Davis, "Melville's Ornamentation: On Irrelevant Beauty," in Samuel Otter and Geoffrey Sanborn, eds., *Melville and Aesthetics* (New York, NY: Palgrave Macmillan, 2011), 34.

14. James, *A Pluralistic Universe*, 129. "Particularly crucial," Theo Davis argues, is that ornamentation can be used to "confer and mark value, without containing an account or representation of what it is that is thereby valued. Also critical is the way that ornamental art adorns and moves within the temporal world, rather than transcending it as pure form or being grounded within it as utter materiality" (*Ornamental Aesthetics: The Poetry of Attending in Thoreau, Dickinson, and Whitman* [New York, NY: Oxford University Press, 2016], 19).

15. Melville, "Cock-a-Doodle-Doo! Or, The Crowing of the Noble Cock Beneventano," in Bryant, *Tales*, 106 (emphasis added). Subsequent references will be to this edition and will be cited parenthetically.

16. Graham Harman, *Heidegger Explained: From Phenomenon to Thing* (Chicago, IL: Open Court, 2007), 1.

17. Melville, "John Marr," in Bryant, *Tales*, 393. Subsequent references will be to this edition and will be cited parenthetically.

18. Elizabeth Grosz, *The Nick of Time: Politics, Evolution, and the Untimely* (Durham, NC: Duke University Press, 2004), 173.

19. Ibid.

20. Graham Harman, "On the Undermining of Objects: Grant, Bruno, and Radical Philosophy," in Levi Bryant, Nick Srnicek, and Graham Harman, eds., *The Speculative Turn: Continental Materialism and Realism* (Melbourne: re.press, 2011), 22.

21. Henry David Thoreau, *Walden* (New York, NY: Signet, 1999), 127.

9 CAMP MELVILLE

1. For the sources of these extracts, see Higgins and Parker, *Herman Melville*, 360, 410, 403, 370, 353, 393, 388, 378, 379, 359, 382, 412, 414, 386.

2. Most of the reviews that mention the book's impiety do so extremely briefly and in a spirit of regretfulness or disapproval, as opposed to a spirit of outright condemnation. Only twelve out of nearly one hundred mention it at all; they are the reviews in the London *John Bull*, the *Albany Argus*, the *New Haven Palladium*, the *New York Independent*, the *New York Christian Inquirer*, the *Literary World*, the *New York Commercial Advertiser*, the *New York Churchman*, the *Washington National Intelligencer*, the *Church Review*, the *Methodist Quarterly Review*, and *To-Day*, in Higgins and Parker, *Herman Melville*, 357–8, 374, 376, 379–80, 382, 384–6, 388, 394–5, 398–401, 409–10, 411, 412–13.

3. Even in the positive reviews, the extravagance of the book came in for criticism. See, for example, the reviews in the *London Morning Post* ("despite its occasional extravagancies, it is a book of extraordinary merit"), the *London Leader* ("there is Nature here, though the daring imagery often grows riotously extravagant"), the *Illustrated London News* ("[he has a] great aptitude for quaint and original philosophical speculation, degenerating however, too often into rhapsody and purposeless extravagance"), and the *London Weekly News and Chronicle* ("the blemish of the book is its occasional extravagance and exaggeration – faults which mar the effect they were intended to heighten") in Higgins and Parker, *Herman Melville*, 372–3, 370–2, 364, 388–90.

4. For the full texts of these three reviews, which appeared in *Graham's Magazine*, the *London Atlas*, and *Bentley's Miscellany*, respectively, see Higgins and Parker, *Herman Melville*, 415, 360–4, 408–9.

5. Eve Kosofsky Sedgwick, *Touching Feeling: Affect, Pedagogy, Performativity* (Durham, NC: Duke University Press, 2003), 137.

6. Ibid., 149.

7. Ibid., 149, 150.

8. Ibid., 150–1.

9. Christopher Castiglia, *Interior States: Institutional Consciousness and the Inner Life of Democracy* (Durham, NC: Duke University Press, 2008), 14.

10. Jennifer Doyle, *Sex Objects: Art and the Dialectics of Desire* (Minneapolis, MN: University of Minnesota Press, 2006), xxx.

11. Ibid., xxxi.
12. Sedgwick, *Tendencies*, 3.
13. Phillips, *The Beast in the Nursery*, 3–4.
14. Review of *Typee, Washington National Intelligencer*, in Higgins and Parker, *Herman Melville*, 73.
15. Eric Auerbach, *Mimesis: The Representation of Reality in Western Thought*, trans. Willard R. Trask (Princeton, NJ: Princeton University Press, 1953), 552.

10 COURTING SURPRISE

1. Hannah Arendt, *Eichmann in Jerusalem: A Report on the Banality of Evil* (New York, NY: Penguin, 1987), 26.
2. Ibid., 49.
3. Ibid., 48, 49.
4. Ibid., 49.
5. Hannah Arendt, *The Life of the Mind* (London: Harcourt, 1971), 5.
6. Ibid., 171.
7. Ibid., 191.
8. Ibid., 174.
9. Hannah Arendt, "Some Questions Concerning Moral Philosophy," in *Responsibility and Judgment* (New York, NY: Schocken, 2003), 100.
10. Ibid., 101.
11. Ibid.
12. Hannah Arendt, *The Jewish Writings* (New York, NY: Schocken, 2007), 479.
13. Ibid.
14. Arendt, *The Life of the Mind*, 176.
15. The marginal comment may be found at *Melville's Marginalia Online* alongside the "Life of Milton" that is included in Milton's *Poetical Works*, 1: xcx.
16. James, *The Principles of Psychology*, 1: 255.
17. Henry James, preface to *Roderick Hudson* (New York, NY: Scribner's, 1907), vii.
18. Toni Morrison, *The Bluest Eye* (New York, NY: Plume, 1984), 48.
19. Ibid.
20. Ibid., 49.
21. James Fenimore Cooper, *The Pioneers* (New York, NY: Penguin, 1988), 82, 86.

22. Harriet Beecher Stowe, *Dred: A Tale of the Great Dismal Swamp* (New York, NY: Penguin, 2000), 198.
23. Arendt, *The Life of the Mind*, 177 (emphasis in original).
24. Arendt, "Personal Responsibility Under Dictatorship," 45 (emphasis in original).
25. Arendt, *The Life of the Mind*, 177; Arendt, *Eichmann in Jerusalem*, 288. Unsurprisingly, perhaps, but also disappointingly, Arendt's thinking didn't carry her very far past the typical anti-black racism of her day. "What the damning evidence of Arendt's anti-black racism shows," Kevin Gaines writes, "is that her 'thinking' on race is infected by a prejudice about which she failed to think; her work failed to confront the difficulty of race on the very terms she establishes for thought" ("Anti-Black Racism in Arendt and Philosophy's Dangerous Commitment to Purity," *Blog of the APA*, July 7, 2016, https://blog.apaonline.org/2016/07/07/anti-black-racism-in-arendt-and-philosophys-dangerous-commitment-to-purity/).
26. Some of the most powerful conceptualizations of this type of anti-racism may be found in the work of James Baldwin and Paul Gilroy. "To be sensual," Baldwin writes, "is to respect and rejoice in the force of life, of life itself, and to be *present* in all that one does, from the effort of loving to the breaking of bread." It is the inability "on the part of white American men and women … to renew themselves at the fountain of their own lives, that makes the discussion, let alone elucidation, of any conundrum – that is, any reality – so supremely difficult" (*The Fire Next Time*, 311–12 [emphasis in original]). "The challenge of being in the same present provides some help in seeing how we might invent conceptions of humanity that allow for the presumption of equal value and go beyond the issue of tolerance into a more active engagement with the irreducible value of diversity within sameness," Gilroy writes. "This cosmopolitan attachment finds civic and ethical value in the process of exposure to otherness. It glories in the ordinary virtues and ironies – listening, looking, discretion, friendship – that can be cultivated when mundane encounters with difference become rewarding" (*Postcolonial Melancholia* [New York, NY: Columbia University Press, 2005], 67).
27. The best psychoanalytic account of the pathological consequences of not-thinking may be found in the work of Wilfred Bion, who argues that "[i]f the patient cannot 'think' with his thoughts, that is to say that he has thoughts but lacks the apparatus of 'thinking' which enables him to use his thoughts," then the patient "is incapable of … learning from experience. This failure is serious.… Failure to eat,

drink or breathe properly has disastrous consequences for life itself. Failure to use emotional experience produces a comparable disaster in the development of the personality" (*Learning from Experience* [London: Karnac, 1984], 85, 56, 42).

28. James, *The Principles of Psychology*, 1: 255–6.
29. Ibid., 1: 254 (emphasis in original).
30. Stern, *Unformulated Experience*, 250.
31. James Breslin, *William Carlos Williams: An American Artist* (New York, NY: Oxford University Press, 1970), 43 (emphasis in original).

11   ALL THINGS TRYING

1. Philip Davis, *Reading and the Reader* (New York, NY: Oxford University Press, 2013), 2.
2. Charles Olson, "The Materials and Weights of Herman Melville," in Donald Allen and Benjamin Friedlander, eds., *Collected Prose* (Berkeley and Los Angeles, CA: University of California Press, 1997), 117.
3. Olson, "Equal, That Is, to the Real Itself," 121.
4. Ibid.
5. Hurston, *Their Eyes Were Watching God*, 90.
6. Herman Melville, "The Apple-Tree Table," in Harrison Hayford, Alma A. MacDougall, and G. Thomas Tanselle, eds., *The Piazza Tales and Other Prose Pieces* (Evanston and Chicago, IL: Northwestern University Press/Newberry Library, 1987), 389.
7. Gilles Deleuze, *Nietzsche and Philosophy*, trans. Hugh Tomlinson (New York, NY: Columbia University Press, 2006), 56.
8. Gerard Manley Hopkins, "As kingfishers catch fire, dragonflies dráw flame," lines 3–8. For more extended versions of this argument about Melville's intense relationship to human and nonhuman "trying," see my "Melville and the Nonhuman World," 10–21, and my *Whipscars and Tattoos: The Last of the Mohicans, Moby-Dick, and the Maori* (New York, NY: Oxford University Press, 2011), 93–131.
9. Herman Melville, "Venice," in Robert C. Ryan, Harrison Hayford, Alma A. MacDougall, and G. Thomas Tanselle, eds., *Published Poems* (Evanston and Chicago, IL: Northwestern University Press/Newberry Library, 2009), 291; Melville, "Statues in Rome," 406.

10. Deleuze, "On Philosophy," quoted in Ronald Bogue, *Deleuze's Wake: Tributes and Tributaries* (Albany, NY: State University of New York Press, 2004), 9.

11. Ralph Waldo Emerson, "Self-Reliance," in *Essays and Lectures* (New York, NY: Library of America, 1983), 271.

12. Deleuze, *Nietzsche and Philosophy*, 40.

13. Herman Melville, *Omoo* (New York, NY: Penguin, 2007), 29.

14. In Melville's best-known celebration of the variegated "array" of humanity, he declares that "[t]here is something in the contemplation of the mode in which America has been settled, that, in a noble breast, should forever extinguish the prejudices of national dislike.... [O]ur blood is as the flood of the Amazon, made up of a thousand noble currents all pouring into one. We are not a nation, so much as a world" (*R*, 195–6).

15. Arendt, *Eichmann in Jerusalem*, 268–9.

16. Melville, "The Paradise of Bachelors and the Tartarus of Maids," in Bryant, *Tales*, 162.

17. Ibid., 165, 159. On the story's painfully clear allegorical level, the added implication of this scenario is that women, in general, are in thrall to reproductivity as such, to the "inevitability" of its "evolvement power" (165). After exactly nine minutes in the machine, in which it "grow[s] more and more to final firmness," the "white, wet, woolly looking" pulp is converted into "foolscap"; there is a "scissory sound ... as of some cord being snapped," and down drops "a sheet of blank paper; something destined to be scribbled on, but what sort of characters no soul might tell" (164, 162, 164, 165).

18. Ibid., 165.

19. He is especially sensitized to the operations of reactive forces in prisons ("How feeble is all language to describe the horrors we inflict upon these wretches, whom we mason up in the cells of our prisons, and condemn to perpetual solitude in the very heart of our population") (*T*, 127) and poverty-zoned spaces ("Of all the preposterous assumptions of humanity over humanity, nothing exceeds most of the criticisms made on the habits of the poor by the well-housed, well-warmed, and well-fed") ("Poor Man's Pudding and Rich Man's Crumbs," in *The Piazza Tales*, 296).

20. Melville, "The Piazza," in *The Piazza Tales*, 9.

21. Ibid., 12.

22. Hannah Arendt, *The Human Condition* (Chicago, IL: University of Chicago Press, 1958), 57, 58.

23. Wilfred Bion, *Attention and Interpretation* (London: Routledge, 2001), 19, 9.

24. James Baldwin, interview with Malcolm Preston, in *Conversations with James Baldwin*, eds. Fred L. Standley and Louis H. Pratt (Jackson, MS: University Press of Mississippi, 1989), 26.

25. James Baldwin, "Mass Culture and the Creative Artist: Some Personal Notes," in Randall Kenan, ed., *The Cross of Redemption: Uncollected Writings* (New York, NY: Vintage, 2011), 6; Baldwin, *The Fire Next Time*, 311.

26. Baldwin, interview with James Mossman, in *Conversations with James Baldwin*, 48.

12 THE NONCOMMUNICATING CENTRAL SELF

1. D. W. Winnicott, "Communicating and Not Communicating Leading to a Study of Certain Opposites," in *The Maturational Processes and the Facilitating Environment* (London: Karnac, 1990), 192, 187.

2. Ibid., 187.

3. Ibid., 192.

4. Herman Melville, *Billy Budd, Sailor*, eds. Harrison Hayford and Merton M. Sealts, Jr., (Chicago, IL: University of Chicago Press, 1962), 53. Subsequent references will be to this edition and will be cited parenthetically with the abbreviation *BB*.

5. Melville, "Shiloh: A Requiem (April 1862)," in Bryant, *Tales*, 344.

6. Michael Warner, "What Like a Bullet Can Undeceive?" *Public Culture* 15 (2003), 49–50.

7. Ibid., 52.

8. Ibid., 52–3.

9. Warner, "What Like a Bullet," 52.

10. In the standard edition of *Billy Budd*, the final sentence of this passage in the manuscript – "Those lights of human intelligence losing human expression, gelidly protruding like the alien eyes of certain uncatalogued creatures of the deep" – is, by means of a "were" inserted before "gelidly," made syntactically complete, in an odd act of editorial resistance to Melville's compositional habit of slipping, once he is deep in a description, out of subject–verb structures.

11. Ezra Pound, "Vorticism," *Fortnightly Review*, September 1914.

12. Woolf, *To the Lighthouse*, 161.

13. Nathaniel Hawthorne, *The English Notebooks, 1856–1860*, eds. Thomas Woodson and Bill Ellis (Columbus, OH: Ohio State University Press, 1997), 163.
14. The comment may be found at *Melville's Marginalia Online* in Milton's *Poetical Works*, 2: 133.
15. Winnicott, "The Capacity to Be Alone," 34.
16. Ibid.
17. Shakespeare, *The Tempest*, 3.2.137–8.

Works Cited

Altieri, Charles. *The Particulars of Rapture: An Aesthetics of the Affects*. Ithaca, NY: Cornell University Press, 2003.

Arendt, Hannah. *Eichmann in Jerusalem: A Report on the Banality of Evil*. New York, NY: Penguin, 1987.

Responsibility and Judgment. New York, NY: Schocken, 2003.

The Jewish Writings. New York, NY: Schocken, 2007.

The Life of the Mind. London: Harcourt, 1971.

Auerbach, Eric. *Mimesis: The Representation of Reality in Western Thought*, trans. Willard R. Trask. Princeton, NJ: Princeton University Press, 1953.

Baldwin, James. *Collected Essays*. New York, NY: Library of America, 1998.

Conversations with James Baldwin, eds. Fred L. Standley and Louis H. Pratt. Jackson, MS: University Press of Mississippi, 1989.

The Cross of Redemption: Uncollected Writings. ed. Randall Kenan. New York, NY: Vintage, 2011.

Becke, Louis. "Introduction." *Moby-Dick*. London: Putnam's, 1901.

Benjamin, Walter. *Illuminations*, trans. Harry Zohn. New York, NY: Schocken, 1968.

Berthoff, Warner. *The Example of Melville*. New York, NY: Norton, 1972.

Bion, Wilfred. *Attention and Interpretation*. London: Routledge, 2001.

Learning from Experience. London: Karnac, 1984.

Blake, William. *The Marriage of Heaven and Hell*. New York, NY: Dover, 1994.

Bogue, Ronald. *Deleuze's Wake: Tributes and Tributaries*. Albany, NY: State University of New York Press, 2004.

Bollas, Christopher. *Being a Character: Psychoanalysis and Self Experience*. New York, NY: Hill and Wang, 1992.

Cracking Up: The Work of Unconscious Experience. New York, NY: Hill and Wang, 1995.

Forces of Destiny: Psychoanalysis and Human Idiom. London: Free Association Books, 1989.

The Evocative Object World. New York, NY: Routledge, 2009.

The Freudian Moment. London: Karnac, 2007.

The Shadow of the Object: Psychoanalysis of the Unthought Known. New York, NY: Columbia University Press, 1987.

Boulanger, Ghislaine. *Wounded by Reality: Understanding and Treating Adult Onset Trauma*. New York, NY: Psychology Press, 2007.

Braidotti, Rosi. *Nomadic Theory: The Portable Rosi Braidotti*. New York, NY: Columbia University Press, 2011.

Breslin, James. *William Carlos Williams: An American Artist*. New York, NY: Oxford University Press, 1970.

Castiglia, Christopher. *Interior States: Institutional Consciousness and the Inner Life of Democracy*. Durham, NC: Duke University Press, 2008.

Cooper, James Fenimore. *The Pioneers*. New York, NY: Penguin, 1988.

Dana, Richard Henry, Jr. *Two Years Before the Mast*. New York, NY: Penguin, 1981.

Davis, Philip. *Reading and the Reader*. New York, NY: Oxford University Press, 2013.

Davis, Theo. "Melville's Ornamentation: On Irrelevant Beauty," in *Melville and Aesthetics*, eds. Samuel Otter and Geoffrey Sanborn. New York, NY: Palgrave Macmillan, 2011.

Ornamental Aesthetics: The Poetry of Attending in Thoreau, Dickinson, and Whitman. New York, NY: Oxford University Press, 2016.

Dayan, Colin. "Melville's Creatures, or Seeing Otherwise," in *American Impersonal: Essays with Sharon Cameron*, ed. Branka Arsic. New York, NY: Bloomsbury, 2014.

Deleuze, Gilles. *Nietzsche and Philosophy*, trans. Hugh Tomlinson. New York, NY: Columbia University Press, 2006.

Dewey, John. *Art as Experience*. New York, NY: Perigree, 2005.

Democracy and Education. New York, NY: Macmillan, 1916.

Downes, Paul. "Melville's Benito Cereno and the Politics of Humanitarian Intervention," *South Atlantic Quarterly* 103 (2004): 465–88.

Doyle, Jennifer. *Sex Objects: Art and the Dialectics of Desire*. Minneapolis, MN: University of Minnesota Press, 2006.

Dryden, Edgar A. *Monumental Melville: The Formation of a Literary Career*. Stanford, CA: Stanford University Press, 2004.

Eigen, Michael. *The Electrified Tightrope*. London: Karnac, 2004.

Emerson, Ralph Waldo. *Essays and Lectures*. New York, NY: Library of America, 1983.

Felski, Rita. *The Limits of Critique*. Chicago, IL: University of Chicago Press, 2015.

Freeburg, Christopher. *Melville and the Idea of Blackness: Race and Imperialism in Nineteenth-Century America*. New York, NY: Cambridge University Press, 2012.

Freud, Sigmund. "Recommendations to Physicians Practicing Psycho-analysis," in *The Freud Reader*, ed. Peter Gay. New York, NY: Norton, 1989.

Gaines, Kevin. "Anti-Black Racism in Arendt and Philosophy's Dangerous Commitment to Purity." *Blog of the APA*, July 7, 2016. https://blog.apaonline.org/2016/07/07/anti-black-racism-in-arendt-and-philosophys-dangerous-commitment-to-purity/.

Gilroy, Paul. *Postcolonial Melancholia*. New York, NY: Columbia University Press, 2005.

Goldberg, Shari. *Quiet Testimony: A Theory of Witnessing from Nineteenth-Century American Literature*. New York, NY: Fordham University Press, 2013.

Grosz, Elizabeth. *Becoming Undone: Darwinian Reflections on Life, Politics, and Art*. Durham, NC: Duke University Press, 2011.

The Nick of Time: Politics, Evolution, and the Untimely. Durham, NC: Duke University Press, 2004.

Harman, Graham. *Heidegger Explained: From Phenomenon to Thing*. Chicago, IL: Open Court, 2007.

"On the Undermining of Objects: Grant, Bruno, and Radical Philosophy," in *The Speculative Turn: Continental Materialism and Realism*, eds. Levi Bryant, Nick Srnicek, and Graham Harman. Melbourne: re.press, 2011.

Hawthorne, Julian. *Nathaniel Hawthorne and His Wife*, 2 vols. Boston, MA: Houghton Mifflin, 1893.

Hawthorne, Nathaniel. *Tales and Sketches*. New York, NY: Library of America, 1982.

The English Notebooks, 1856–1860, eds. Thomas Woodson and Bill Ellis. Columbus, OH: Ohio State University Press, 1997.

Heaney, Seamus. *The Redress of Poetry*. New York, NY: Farrar, Straus, & Giroux, 1995.

Higgins, Brian and Hershel Parker, eds. *Herman Melville: The Contemporary Reviews*. New York, NY: Cambridge University Press, 1995.

Hoover, Bob. "'Hard Books,' Easy Lessons from Oprah." *Pittsburgh Post-Gazette*, July 9, 2006.

Hopkins, Gerard Manley. "Journal Entry." in *Gerard Manley Hopkins: The Major Works*, ed. Catherine Phillips. New York, NY: Oxford University Press, 2002.

Hurston, Zora Neale. *Their Eyes Were Watching God*. New York, NY: Harper, 2006.

James, Henry. *Roderick Hudson*. New York, NY: Scribner's, 1907.

James, William. *A Pluralistic Universe*. Cambridge: Harvard University Press, 1977.

The Principles of Psychology. 2 vols. New York, NY: Dover, 1950.

Kazin, Alfred. "Introduction," in *Melville: A Collection of Critical Essays*, ed. Richard Chase. Englewood Cliffs, NJ: Prentice Hall, 1962.

Kleist, Heinrich von. "On the Gradual Fabrication of Thoughts While Speaking," in *An Abyss Deep Enough: Letters of Heinrich von Kleist with a Selection of Essays and Anecdotes*, ed. Philip B. Miller. New York, NY: Dutton, 1982.

Knight, G. Wilson. *The Wheel of Fire: Interpretations of Shakespearean Tragedy*. New York, NY: Oxford University Press, 1930.

Lauter, Paul. *From Walden Pond to Jurassic Park: Activism, Culture, and American Studies*. Durham, NC: Duke University Press, 2001.

Lee, Maurice. "Melville's Subversive Political Philosophy: 'Benito Cereno' and the Fate of Speech," *American Literature* 72 (2000): 495–519.

Leonard, James S., Thomas Tenney, and Thadious M. Davis, eds. *Satire or Evasion? Black Perspectives on Huckleberry Finn*. Durham, NC: Duke University Press, 1991.

Mandel, Ruth. "The Two Mystery Stories in 'Benito Cereno,'" *Texas Studies in Literature and Language* 24 (1973): 631–42.

Martin, Terry. "The Idea of Nature in Benito Cereno." *Studies in Short Fiction* 30 (1993): 161–68.

Matthiessen, F. O. *American Renaissance: Art and Expression in the Age of Emerson and Whitman*. New York, NY: Oxford University Press, 1941.

McCall, Dan. *The Silence of Bartleby*. Ithaca, NY: Cornell University Press, 1989.

McCarthy, Cormac. *The Road*. New York, NY: Vintage, 2006.

Melville, Herman. *Billy Budd, Sailor*. eds. Harrison Hayford and Merton M. Sealts, Jr.. Chicago, IL: University of Chicago Press, 1962.

Clarel, eds. Harrison Hayford, Alma A. MacDougall, Hershel Parker, and G. Thomas Tanselle. Evanston and Chicago, IL: Northwestern University Press/Newberry Library, 1991.

Correspondence, ed. Lynn Horth. Evanston and Chicago, IL: Northwestern University Press/Newberry Library, 1993.

Journals, eds. Howard C. Horsford and Lynn Horth. Evanston and Chicago, IL: Northwestern University Press/Newberry Library, 1989.

Mardi. Evanston, IL: Northwestern University Press, 1998.

Moby-Dick. New York, NY: Norton, 2002.

Omoo. New York, NY: Penguin, 2007.

Pierre. New York, NY: Penguin, 1996.

Published Poems, eds. Robert C. Ryan, Harrison Hayford, Alma A. MacDougall, and G. Thomas Tanselle. Evanston and Chicago, IL: Northwestern University Press/Newberry Library, 2009.

Redburn. New York, NY: Modern Library, 2002.

Tales, Poems, and Other Writings, ed. John Bryant. New York, NY: Modern Library, 2001.

The Confidence-Man. New York, NY: Penguin, 1990.

The Piazza Tales and Other Prose Pieces, eds. Harrison Hayford, Alma A. MacDougall, and G. Thomas Tanselle. Evanston and Chicago, IL: Northwestern University Press/Newberry Library, 1987.

Typee. Boston, MA: Houghton Mifflin, 2004.

White-Jacket. Evanston, IL: Northwestern University Press, 2000.

Milner, Marion. *On Not Being Able to Paint*. London: Routledge, 2010.

The Hands of the Living God. London: Hogarth, 1969.

Morrison, Toni. *Beloved*. New York, NY: Vintage, 2004.

The Bluest Eye. New York, NY: Plume, 1984.

"This Amazing, Troubling Book," in *Ethics, Literature and Theory: An Introductory Reader*, ed. Stephen K. George. Lanham, MD: Rowman and Littlefield, 2005.

Olson, Charles. *Collected Prose*, eds. Donald Allen and Benjamin Friedlander. Berkeley and Los Angeles, CA: University of California Press, 1997.

Otter, Samuel. "Reading *Moby-Dick*," in *The New Cambridge Companion to Herman Melville*, ed. Robert S. Levine. New York, NY: Cambridge University Press, 2014.

Ozick, Cynthia. "Judging the World." *New York Times Book Review*, March 13, 2014.

Phillips, Adam. *Equals*. New York, NY: Basic Books, 2002.

On Flirtation. Cambridge: Harvard University Press, 1994.

The Beast in the Nursery: On Curiosity and Other Thoughts. New York, NY: Vintage, 1998.

Plath, Sylvia. *The Journals of Sylvia Plath*. New York, NY: Anchor, 1998.

Poe, Edgar Allan. *Essays and Reviews*. New York, NY: Library of America, 1984.

Pound, Ezra. "Vorticism." *Fortnightly Review*, September 1914.

Robinson, Marilynne. *Gilead*. New York, NY: Picador, 2004.

Housekeeping. New York, NY: Farrar, Straus, and Giroux, 1980.

Sanborn, Geoffrey. "Melville and the Nonhuman World," in *The New Cambridge Companion to Herman Melville*, ed. Robert S. Levine. Cambridge: Cambridge University Press, 2014.

The Sign of the Cannibal: Melville and the Making of a Postcolonial Reader. Durham, NC: Duke University Press, 1998.

"The Tale That Won't Let Go," *O Magazine* (July 2006), 164.

Whipscars and Tattoos: The Last of the Mohicans, Moby-Dick, and the Maori. New York, NY: Oxford University Press, 2011.

Savage, Elizabeth. "What We Talk Around When We Talk About The Dick." *Feminist Teacher* 21 (2011): 95–6.

Schwartz, Lloyd and Sybil P. Estess, eds. *Elizabeth Bishop and Her Art.* Ann Arbor, MI: University of Michigan Press, 1983.

Sedgwick, Eve Kosofsky. *Tendencies.* Durham, NC: Duke University Press, 1993.

Touching Feeling: Affect, Pedagogy, Performativity. Durham, NC: Duke University Press, 2003.

Stern, Donnell. *Unformulated Experience: From Dissociation to Imagination in Psychoanalysis.* New York, NY: Psychology Press, 2003.

Stowe, Harriet Beecher. *Dred: A Tale of the Great Dismal Swamp.* New York, NY: Penguin, 2000.

Tamarkin, Elisa. "Melville with Pictures," in *The New Cambridge Companion to Herman Melville*, ed. Robert S. Levine. New York, NY: Cambridge University Press, 2014.

Thoreau, Henry David. *Walden.* New York, NY: Signet, 1999.

Wallace, David Foster. *Infinite Jest.* New York, NY: Little, Brown, 1996.

Warner, Michael. "What Like a Bullet Can Undeceive?" *Public Culture* 15 (2003): 49–50.

Williams, Raymond. *The Long Revolution.* New York, NY: Harper & Row, 1961.

Willis, Nathaniel Parker. *Hurry-Graphs; or, Sketches of Scenery, Celebrities and Society, Taken from Life.* Auburn, AL and Rochester, NY: Alden and Beardsley, 1856.

Winnicott, D. W. *Playing and Reality.* London: Routledge, 1991.

The Maturational Processes and the Facilitating Environment. London: Karnac, 1990.

Winters, Yvor. *Maule's Curse: Seven Studies in the History of American Obscurantism.* Norfolk, CT: New Directions, 1938.

Woolf, Virginia. *To the Lighthouse.* New York, NY: Harcourt, 1927.

Yeats, William Butler. *Selected Poems and Three Plays*, ed. M. L. Rosenthal. New York, NY: Macmillan, 1962.

Index

Printed in the United States
by Baker & Taylor Publisher Services